IT'S A CONTINUUM

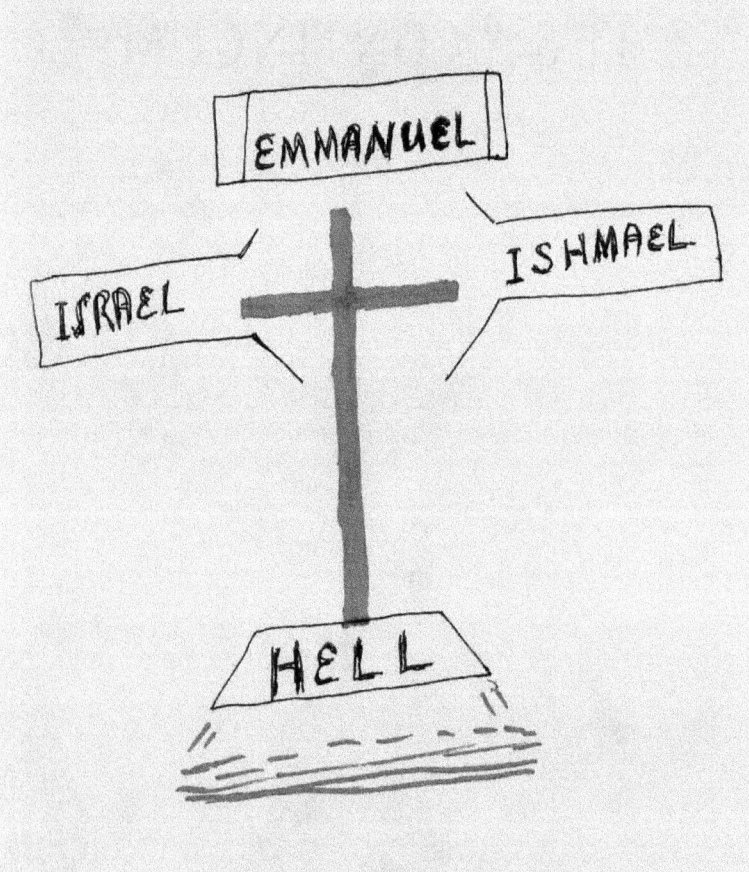

IT'S A CONTINUUM

FOR THERE IS NO OTHER NAME!—Acts 4:12

Leo Emmanuel Lochard

RESOURCE *Publications* · Eugene, Oregon

IT'S A CONTINUUM
FOR THERE IS NO OTHER NAME!—Acts 4:12

Copyright © 2019 Leo Emmanuel Lochard. All rights reserved. Except for brief quotations in critical publications or reviews, no part of this book may be reproduced in any manner without prior written permission from the publisher. Write: Permissions, Wipf and Stock Publishers, 199 W. 8th Ave., Suite 3, Eugene, OR 97401.

Resource Publications
An Imprint of Wipf and Stock Publishers
199 W. 8th Ave., Suite 3
Eugene, OR 97401

www.wipfandstock.com

PAPERBACK ISBN: 978-1-5326-7093-0
HARDCOVER ISBN: 978-1-5326-7094-7
EBOOK ISBN: 978-1-5326-7095-4

Manufactured in the U.S.A.   12/18/19

To my parents who taught us the joy of sacrificial love and the depth of Human affection for emotional nourishment. To God who gives us a truly meaningful sense of purpose and fulfillment as we journey throughout our earthly life. To our Lord and Savior Jesus Christ, for empowering us with His Holy Spirit, not only for "life more abundant," but also for eternal life.

*

"I can do all things through Christ who strengthens me."
(Philippians 4:13)

CONTENTS

INTRODUCTION • 1
OUR FRAME OF REFERENCE • 2
LIVING WITH "ENVIRONMENTAL STRESSORS" • 17
RECKONING WITH "OUR PREDICAMENT" • 19
WHY WE NEED TO BE "SAVED?" • 37
HOW DO WE USE OUR FREE WILL? • 49
HUMAN HISTORY FROM THE VIEWPOINT OF A MORTAL! • 77
WHY ONLY JESUS! • 95
THE MEANING OF PURPOSIVE HUMAN LIVING • 113
JESUS MAKES ALL THINGS RIGHT! • 116

INTRODUCTION

"In the beginning God created the heaven and the earth. And the earth was without form, and void; and darkness was upon the face of the deep. And the Spirit of God moved upon the face of the waters. And God said, Let there be light: and there was light. And God saw the light: that it was good. And God divided the light from the darkness. And God called the light Day, and the darkness he called Night." (Genesis 1:1–5, Holy Bible.)

Thus, began our material physical Universe, sum of which, God spoke into being, after which, God created us: Humankind. We work during the Day and rest during the Night. Day is light; and Night is darkness.

"We've heard it all," some people will exclaim. And that can be said about a lot of things. But how about the Name Above All Names?

Many people used to know that Name: the Name of Jesus. They've either forgotten it, grown weary of life's turmoil, or they've gone a little bit "off the track."

Other people have either not been taught about that Name or they've decided not to learn about that Name. And that Name is Jesus Christ, Savior of all Humankind!

Why is the Name of Jesus "above every name?" What is so special about that Name, the Name of Jesus? Why is He Savior of all Humankind?

This expository book will analytically explore those questions, as supported by Scriptures, that is, the Word of God in the Holy Bible.

✳✳✳

OUR FRAME OF REFERENCE

"In the beginning was the Word, and the Word was with God, and the Word was God. The same was in the beginning with God. All things were made by him; and without him was not any thing made that was made. In him was life; and the life was the light of men. And the light shined in the darkness and the darkness comprehended it not." (John 1:1–5, Holy Bible).

And thus began, the spiritual Creation of Humankind by the Word of God who spoke the Light into being. Thus, in God was life. And light proceeds from Life. Light and Darkness were created together; but the Darkness could not understand the Light.

"For God is not a God of confusion, but of peace, as in all the churches of the saints." (1 Corinthians 14:33).

Truth chases out ignorance and love chases out fear. Darkness tends to instill fear due to confusion; as Light tends to instill peace due to clarity.

And love casts out fear, because, in love, there is understanding, and thus, repentance. Peace chases out confusion, because in peace, there is forgiveness, patience and forbearance. (1 John 4:18).

Love, peace, understanding, patience, and forbearance nourish Liberty from which ensues freedom. Freedom brings joy that produces endurance and thus grace!

"Law" is "the right way" to do something "truly real." How do we go from "law" to "grace?"

"For the law was given through Moses, but grace and truth came through Jesus Christ." (John 1:17).

We have to begin "on the same page." Human reasoning alone cannot do genuine credit to God's love for us. But only through the Holy Spirit of God, can we gain a fuller, deeper, and more complete comprehension of our "reasons for living." Otherwise, misunderstandings and misinterpretations might creep in, so as to either drive the message to confusion or to the wrong conclusions.

Did not the Devil deceive Adam and Eve, our Forbears, through "his deceitful reasoning," in order to annul the efficacy or "right working" of the commandment or "law" which God had given them, not to eat of the fruit of the tree of knowledge of good and evil, lest they shall die? (Genesis 2:15–17).

But did God "kill them" because of their disobedience? They did not "die" right away, but became mortal. Mortality came with their commission of the sin of disobedience. Violation of the "law" or "commandment" gave birth to "moral conscience" or the "foreknowledge" of the difference between right and wrong, and between good and evil. They could no longer "stay in the presence of the Lord." For, now, "their eyes were opened." They had gained "understanding." Thus, they "hid from God." (Genesis 2:25; 3:4–5).

What was their "punishment?" God showed or demonstrated how His "loving grace" would "work right" to lead Humankind into the "path of righteousness," in order that the guilt and shame associated with the sin of disobedience might dissipate, so as to give birth to peace, liberty, freedom, patience, endurance, and thus, "prosperity." God showed them Mercy!

But now, they would have to only "pursue a life of travail."

"Cursed is the ground for thy sake; in sorrow shalt thou eat of it all the days of thy life."

"In the sweat of thy face shalt thou eat bread, till thou return unto the ground; for out of it wast thou taken: for dust thou art, and unto dust shalt thou return." (Genesis 3:17–24).

Now that Adam and Eve had eaten out of the tree of knowledge of good and evil, they became mortal, and thus, God prevented them from eating out of the tree of life, which would allow them to live forever.

"And the Lord said, Behold, the man is become as one of us, to know good and evil; and now lest he put forth his hand and take also of the tree of life, and eat and live forever: Therefore the Lord sent him forth from the garden of Eden, to till the ground from whence he was taken."

God made "coats of skins, and clothed them." That was the first "animal sacrifice" as "atonement for sin." (Genesis 3:21). For "life is in the blood." And no person shall eat of it! (Leviticus 17:10)

IT'S A CONTINUUM

"For the life of the flesh is in the blood, and I have given it for you on the altar to make atonement for your souls; for it is the blood that makes atonement, by reason of the life." (Leviticus 17:11).

God did not institute "Human sacrifice" for sin atonement; only pagan cultures had practiced "Human sacrifice" to the false "gods" which they thought they were worshipping. God had another plan for saving Humanity.

"You shall make for yourselves no idols nor graven image, neither rear you up a standing image in your land, neither shall ye set up any image of stone in your land, to bow down unto it. For I am the Lord your God." (Leviticus 26:1)

"Ye shall keep my sabbaths, and reverence my sanctuary." (Leviticus 26:2).

Thus, from the beginning, God had forbidden any erection of stone in the land as "a house for His Spirit," or any engraved image that would "represent Him" on the Earth, but rather commanded the Israelites to show reverence for sabbaths (days of worship) and "my sanctuary."

So, we've decided to begin at the Beginning: The Book of Genesis wherein is proclaimed, the Creation of the whole universe by God, as well as of all life as we know it.

But we will consider the life of Human Beings of primary, first, importance in regards to addressing the questions posed above.

The Holy Bible tells us that after creating Humankind, male and female, in the Garden of Eden, clear and certain were God's instructions to them not to eat of the fruit of the tree of knowledge of good and evil that is at the center of the Garden. But they did eat.

They were deceived by the Devil, Satan, Lucifer who took the beastly form of a Serpent and lied to them by counter-posing another narrative that "finessed" the deadly consequences that God had said would ensue from disobedience of His instructions.

Satan told them that they won't surely die, but that, instead, they will become "like God." (Genesis 3:4–5; Proverbs 12:6; 14:12; 16:25). Thus, from the start, Satan had coveted God's throne as a prize to grasp in order to, himself, rule and lord it over the whole Creation.

Thus, did Humankind "fall from God's grace;" and God cast them out of the Garden as all of the participants received their due punishment, respectively: God instituted Human labor, precautions to safeguard knowledge of "the tree of life," eternal life, that is, as well as established Mortality unto the "existence" of Human Beings, sum of which, to yield humility, prevent arrogance, avert foolhardiness, and therefore, to produce wisdom. (Proverbs 11:2)

God looked at all His creation and it grieved His heart deeply to witness how the character of the deceiver, Satan, had been imprinted upon the minds and hearts of Human Beings whom God had created "unto His own image and likeness." Not only Humans were now sinful by fashioning their behavior to follow the character of Satan, they also became mortal. That means Human Beings now had "a span of life," that is: They lived only for a short time as opposed to "living forever." Human Beings would live: from conception and birth, to development and growth, to maturity and old age, and then, from senility to death.

"For the law brings wrath, but where there is no law there is no transgression." (Romans 4:15).

"Apart from the law sin lies dead." (Romans 7:8)

"For no human being will be justified in His sight by works of the law, since through the law comes knowledge of sin." (Romans 3:20).

After Adam and Eve had eaten of the tree of knowledge of good and evil, "their eyes were opened," and knowing now that they were naked, they covered themselves with "fig leaves" as aprons, and then hid themselves from God's presence. (Genesis 3:7)

But God was gravely concerned about, not only about Adam and Eve's "way of life" that would end in biological death, as mortal Beings, but also about their spiritual destiny, because they were created in His own image and likeness or in "the image and likeness of God." (Genesis 1:26-27).

Though we could no longer "live forever," Human Beings were not simply physical biological Beings. They were also spiritual Beings who, in addition, possessed a Soul; hence, the Scriptures' pronouncement that: "The soul that sinneth shall die." (Ezekiel 18:20).

The soul comprises the mind or intellect, or "the cognitive domain;" the emotions, or feelings, or "the affective domain;" and the will to do, to act, to move, to create and produce or, "the psycho-motor domain."

The Holy Bible tells us that God is the Spirit and where the Spirit of the Lord is, there is liberty; hence, the proscription against making any graven or stone image or other forms of physical representation of God. (2 Corinthians 3:17-18).

Animals that are "lower forms of life" do not possess "free will." They can't know either their own essential nature or their own eternal destiny.

IT'S A CONTINUUM

And they don't have the knowledge of good and evil. Only Human Beings do.

Thus, Human free will sets us apart from the "lower life forms." Animals are genetically designed or "pre-wired," so to speak, to act upon "instinct," or to behave "as programmed by their DNA," without the benefit of free will or of the knowledge of their earth condition or mode of existence. But animals will only execute crude reiterative routines of acting in certain specific ways, under corresponding circumstances, that are "attached" to the specific Species to which they belong. Consequently, animal "actions" are "Species-specific." They do not have free will as we do. Their "instinctual routines," such as "fight or flight," follow specific patterns and sequences of behavior that are akin to the Species to which they belong.

For examples, wolves travel in packs whereby one amongst them is the dominant one over all the others, until displaced by another wolf that challenges its "leading the pack." Wolves devour sheep as prey. Hence, the need for a Shepherd to guide and protect the sheep.

Bees have queens whose "leadership patterns" imitate those of the wolf pack, in addition, to "specializing" in "making honey." Everywhere on the earth, "honey bees" will engage in "making honey" in accordance with the "wired instinctual instructions" that already predispose them to "make honey" at infinitum until death.

But, though Human Beings also display reiterative patterns of behavior, such as eating, sleeping, reproducing, etc . . . , that are also considered "genetic predispositions," however, because they have freedom of volition, Humans also have the liberty to decide which actions they will take. God is Spirit and where the Spirit of the Lord is there is liberty, hence, having "the image and likeness of God" our Creator is the only Source of our freedoms. (2 Corinthians 3:17–18).

Such free will characteristics or freedom of volition, does not belong to the lower species of animals that, as long as they exist, continue to exhibit the same patterns and sequences of behavior, as required per certain specific conditions, that are both environmentally and genetically predetermined. Hence, God's commandments against making graven images resembling animals or erections of stone pillars.

But did not Aaron the priest "mess up" by letting the children of Israel build a "golden calf?" Hence, why God will change the priesthood!

Given that we were created in the image and likeness of God, we have certain characteristic gifts or endowments akin to those of our Creator.

We have the predisposition to think freely, that is, without hindrance or compulsion. We own a range of emotions or feelings that are sometimes "sensitively dependent" upon circumstances we have to deal with.

But because we do have free will, we can also decide how we will respond to situations we encounter in life. Love is more than a mere "feeling." True love is a willful act of making a decision to "do the Truth in love."

"Abraham believed God and it was reckoned to him as righteousness." (Genesis 15:6; 21:12; Romans 4:4; 9:7; Hebrews 11:18).

We observe that, more and more, God would expect Humans to reflect His character-qualities and abstract endowments that focused their attention away from the flesh to rather concentrate their energies on what is spiritual. Abraham's faith in God was his righteousness; his actions would then only align with the faith in which he had already chosen to believe: He believed God; and thus, obedience followed as an act of free will!

Therefore, because we are "spirit-beings," it is our faith governing our actions, through obedience of God's commandments that gives life to "righteousness" within our hearts.

We are not called to "worship the flesh" or "the human body." The flesh perishes but the spirit lives forever. (John 6:63). For it is only through reflecting "the image and likeness of God" within us that we can relate to each other with love, Mercy, grace, justice, compassion, and charity.

God is one, but we're many; and so different from one another in many ways that cater to external appearance. But God judges us "according to the heart." (1 Samuel 16:7).

"But the LORD said unto Samuel, Look not on his countenance, or on the height of his stature; because I have refused him: for *the LORD seeth* not as man seeth; for man looketh on the outward appearance, but the LORD looketh on the heart."

Did Satan use force or violence against Adam and Eve; or did he use "convincing words" that persuaded them "from the heart," to disobey, rather than obey God's commands?

But, contrarily, Satan had not remained "as an angel" during this devious act of deception. He took "physical form" in order to "access the hearts" of Adam and Eve. It was therefore a "spiritual deception" rather than a forceful act of compulsory submission.

Satan had become a Serpent in Eden. But Christ Jesus became a Man. (Philippians 2:5–8).

IT'S A CONTINUUM

Christ embodied "the image and likeness of God" as well as "the heart of God." His thoughts and actions, both, reflected the intrinsic character of His heavenly Father, our heavenly Father, Almighty God. (Mark 6:34; 10:18; Colossians 1:15–20). Thus, though Christ became a Man, He was also "God in the flesh!" Hence, why He rose from the dead as prophesied! (John 1:1–14). Only by taking the form of a Man, a Human Being, like us, could Jesus freely entreat us to follow Him from heartfelt conviction by faith. (Philippians 2:9–11).

From the start then, God had showed compassion for our Humanity, and love for God in us in the form of His own image and likeness, by approaching us with the same image He possessed, that of the Father, rather than "the image of the beast." (John 14: 6–7; Revelation 13:15–18).

What do those things mean ultimately: Freedom of thought, freedom to experience a complex repertoire of emotions; and self-awareness, moral conscience, or our self-conscious acknowledgement of our "free will?"

Here, we are encountering the Soul of Human Beings: Whereas animals "adapt to their environment," Human Beings spiritually frame their living existence, in ways that are independent of environmental conditions, or of Species-specific, "genetically wired" forms of behavioral actions.

We can "transform the environment" to accommodate our desires, for the fulfillment of our needs. Beneficent transformation of our environment also hinges upon our converted hearts and transformed minds unto God's ways of righteousness rather than from our clinging to "the image of the beast," thus resulting in destruction, chaos, violence, and death. (Romans 12:1–2; 1 Corinthians 2:16).

For example, we can choose when we go to sleep or when we eat; we invent and design machines that can change the temperature of our dwellings, in response to seasonal variations. In Summer, we utilize "air conditioning;" and in the Winter, heat from an equipment designed for "temperature control," a manufactured furnace.

God did not "take the lives" of our "Eden ancestors" when they sinned. Nor did they die immediately; but they did inherit mortality. Eventually, intrinsic to our biological genetic design, is the termination of our lives, otherwise called "death."

Human Beings were free from the beginning, first from sin, and thus, from guilt or condemnation. Hence God's plan to restore His relationship with us through Christ Jesus whose blood cleanses us from all sin,

OUR FRAME OF REFERENCE

and therefore, erases our guilt and blots out our condemnation. (Romans 8:1–11).

But that had changed when our "Garden ancestors," Adam and Eve, disobeyed God's commandment. Innocence, once lost, could not be "regained;" but only tempered with self-control which we obtain from hearing and doing God's Word through principles of righteous faith given to us by Christ under the New Covenant of love and peace, Mercy and grace. (2 Timothy 1:7).

Even when casting them out of the Garden, God did not abolish, nor extinguish their freewill. God had gifted them with liberty, since from the time of Creation, but, which they chose to exercise against God's instructions, due to the devil's deceitful lies that contradicted the edicts, laid down by God regarding the deadly consequences of deliberate disobedience.

We are certain then, that, Human liberty did not randomly emerge, or accidentally sprout, from "environmental adaptations," sums of which, have not abated unto dissolution, nor disappeared, nor ceased.

Given that, even after presumably "billions of years of evolution," we still get bacterial and viral infections; we must drink water when thirsty, lest we dehydrate, or become eventually desiccated. We've not "evolved" into "another Species" for which we would then become "biological missing links," as professed by Evolutionists. Apes are still here with us on the Earth; nor have they "evolved" into any intelligent forms of life above the lower animals.

Nor did Human Liberty anarchically proceed from experiences arising without cause, or from randomly occurring phenomena. A chaotic explosion like the so-called "big bang" would disperse Matter and Energy and not coalesce into any form of objects that we call "Stars" and "Planets." From Genesis, and the Prophets, we definitely learn from God's Word, that God did not create us "a chaos," but a well-organized order of structured phenomena proceeding in accordance with intrinsic laws that govern their operations. (Isaiah 45:18–21).

Cause-and-effect is a scientific principle applied in all fields of knowledge, regardless of so-called "random fluctuations" within "the quantum realm." Such "fluctuations," are also due to physical cause-and-effect mechanisms yet to be discovered, e.g., the orbital trajectory or path of a "nearly mass-less," Electron, still possessing "significant mass" for revolving around the atomic nucleus as affected by nano-Gravity-Forces and nano-Electromagnetic-Forces.

IT'S A CONTINUUM

Every "law of Physics" is effectual or applies within a specific range of coverage. Newton's Law of Gravitation could not be continuously extended in application to explain "the perihelion Shift of Planet Mercury;" it took Einstein's Theory of Relativity, which picked-up "where Newton had left off" to explain such a significant orbital Shift.

Thus, even "laws" have limits in their application or range of effective coverage. It is not by accident that the Star in our Solar System can "accommodate" only a specific number of Planets, given the limits controlled by its size, mass, electromagnetic and gravity force exertions.

Because of our having gained "knowledge of good and evil," Human liberty must also be characterized by certain "boundaries" or "limits," which are set by what we call "rules, laws, regulations, or statutes."

Such "regulations" or "laws" guide, instruct, inform, or direct our choices when we must decide the types of actions or kinds of behaviors we can freely engage in.

However, such actions, deeds, works, or behaviors allow us to engage within "a range of freedom" that must conform to those regulated prescriptions or proscriptions, "as applicable by law."

"Laws" must safeguard our liberty while simultaneously determining "the range of behaviors" we can freely and deliberately engage in; that is, according to their prescribed boundaries and limits that encompass their "ranges of freedom."

We have the God-given inalienable "right to own property;" but there are regulated ways that frame our ability to acquire property, justly, peacefully, rightly, and lawfully; that is, without injury or harm to other Human Beings.

"Thou shalt not steal" is the foundation upon which lawful ownership of property is erected. Property can be a free gift to a person, as granted by the owner of that specific property. Property can also be lawfully earned through labor or work for which wages are paid. Property can be inherited from other Human Beings with whom we have certain specific relations, as willed by the owners, or as prescribed by legal determination in a court of law. "Property" can also be lawfully, justly, and peacefully acquired through purchases or sales, or auctions, etc. . .., according to price or cost agreements between sellers and buyers, sums of which, we broadly or generally refer to, as "the Economy." There is always "a right way" to acquire or obtain property, without injury or harm to anyone. Hence why established "laws" must allow equal access to all Human Beings in a society to the numerous lawfully prescribed ways in which "property" can be justly, rightly, and peacefully acquired.

For Scriptures command that: "The earth is the Lord's and the fullness thereof, the world and those who dwell therein; for He has founded it upon the seas, and established it upon the rivers." (Psalms 24:1).

"The earth and everything therein is the Lord's," because we all die eventually, to leave it all behind. "You can't take it with you!" "No U-haul behind a hearse!" (Luke 12:15). In short, we can't "put the Planet in our pockets" and "stake a claim" on it as "ours." By the grace of God who gives us life and liberty: We're "only passing through!"

But, at the same time, we're no longer driven by wickedness that causes us to do evil, for as we are under grace, consciousness of sin through knowledge of good and evil is annulled, in order to bring righteousness through faith.

"For sin will have no dominion over you, since you are not under law but under grace." (Romans 6:14).

We act freely regarding both "genetically wired needs," e.g., we can freely choose when to eat, and "socially necessitated responses" to situations we encounter as we live in society, and on the Earth.

"Society," is, first and foremost, a "shared spiritual environment." Animals don't "make laws." But Human society is governed by those "rules, laws, regulations, or statutes" that guide or direct which actions we can take towards each other, towards things in society, and/or during specific situational events, in order to fulfill our needs, or satisfy our desires, without harm or injury to no one, e.g., when it is raining or snowing, we have the freedom of choice in deciding which garments we'll wear that protect us from the rain or the cold snow; or "with goodwill to all and with malice towards none," we can freely choose to befriend another Human Being or not, without making him or her into "an enemy;" or we can freely decide to deliberately join "an open organization" or "private organization," in accordance with its lawfully, justly, peacefully and freely determined, "prescribed rules, policies, regulations, or procedures," to sum of which, we refer, as "Freedom of Association," e.g., trade unions; local church congregations; political parties, etc. . .

Abraham Lincoln, before he became President of the United States in 1861, gave a speech before the Young Men's Lyceum in Springfield, Illinois, on January 27, 1838, during which, he said:

IT'S A CONTINUUM

"At what point then is the approach of danger to be expected? I answer, if it ever reach us, it must spring up amongst us. It cannot come from abroad. If destruction be our lot, we must ourselves be its author and finisher. As a nation of freemen, we must live through all time, or die by suicide."

God gave us Life and Liberty so that we can engage in "the pursuit of Happiness" in lawful and peaceable ways that edify the beneficent "goods and services" we've accumulated thus far in Human history for our "general welfare." We're one of the most powerful countries in the world, militarily speaking; and thus, no external enemy can invade America to forcefully or violently subdue its population into political bondage or cultural slavery. Therefore, Mr. Lincoln, does "have a point!" WE THE PEOPLE, each and every individual Person living freely in our society is responsible and accountable for every event that takes place therein, thereby impacting other individuals in our society, e.g., crimes of violence, abuse, theft, or murder — barring natural phenomena like tornadoes and hurricanes; unpredictable disasters, like fires and floods; or accidents due to Human error during unforeseen circumstances or unknown conditions, like car accidents or plane crashes during a snow storm, or during some other forms of "non-directed events" that "take a Human toll."

However, many times, in many situations or "frames of circumstances," e.g., which offered job or position to accept; which road or route to take for a certain specific destination, etc..., our choices are seldom "error-free," due to our "fallen nature."

Many factors may input into our freedom of will, during a decision-making process, depending on the parameters or conditions encountered during the deliberate decision-making processes guiding us in making that specific exercise of "free choice."

In addition, God did not change His relationship to us only, but also to the earthly physical environment in which we live. The very ground upon which the Serpent is to crawl all the days of its life is "accursed" by our Creator! (Genesis 3:17).

However, because God's love for us is pure, holy, sinless, and righteous, due to our sinfulness He has only changed the conditions within which or under which we can rightfully "commune with Him." (Hebrews 10:18–25).

God had to have a "plan of salvation" in order to restore our free, righteous, and holy relationships with Him. For then, God could perform "miracles" with our Faith, because His love surpasses or transcends "the strict and just tenor" required of His wrathful holiness. We are to trust In

OUR FRAME OF REFERENCE

God by faith and are saved by faith and not by works; we are not under the Law but under grace, so that no one can boast because of their works. (Ephesians 2:8–10).

But, only Jesus, is the author and finisher or "perfecter of our faith." (Hebrews 12:1–2).

"Therefore it is of faith that it might be by grace; to the end the promise might be sure to all the seed; not to that only which is of the law, but to that also which is of the faith of Abraham; who is the father of us all, (As it is written, I have made thee a father of many nations), before Him whom he believed, even God, who gives life to the dead, and calls into being things that do not exist yet as though they did already." (Romans 4:16–17).

Therefore, here is the crux of our predicament or "Human condition:" We are sinful by nature, on the one hand, and on the other, the Earth itself, or our physical-material, or ecological environment itself, is also subject to "Entropy."

"Entropy," simply states that things that are purposely organized for fulfilling certain specific functions, whether in Nature or in society, if not consciously attended to, will tend to decay, degrade, disrupt, disperse, or end, e.g., a fruit will decay and "return to seed" if not harvested or eaten "at the right time;" we build cars for transportation and they deteriorate to the point of needing "a junk yard" or "salvage yard;" we are conceived and born, to then mature, age, and eventually die.

Thus, "Entropy," is a "naturally unfolding phenomenon" that may be present in almost all situations that involve any process, event, activity, function, or performance, within the framework of "the Law of Transformation" that inheres in this Universe.

Things will repeat in periodic cycles during which they'll process relatively the same variables in order to produce the same outputs, e.g., Seasonal Cycles.

This pattern or template of "reiterative cycling," is consistent with the Law of Energy Transformation. Thermodynamics requires Entropy because physical processes must have a beginning and an end, while preserving Conservation in their duration or during their "life-span." But, as we know, even Energy Transformation has its "limits and boundaries," including the "laws" governing its "scientific operations."

Consequently, from our own characteristic "way of being" as Humans, which we call "Human Nature," we suffer from sinfulness; and from the physical processes intrinsic to the existence of the Earth as a "living Planet,"

IT'S A CONTINUUM

to which we usually refer as "Nature or the natural environment," inhere the "entropic patterns" of decay or degradation, of which, we also partake, due to our biological physiological body that is engineered by our Creator to be subject to the same "entropic patterns of processing" belonging to the course of the natural environment, e.g., we can get bacterial infections that cause fever; we eat, to digest, and dispose of waste matter; and our lives do end eventually, in "death," to be honorably buried in the cemetery of our choice.

From "all frames of reference" that we encounter during our temporary existence on the Earth, we are pummeled by certain "Species-specific deficiencies," such that they can be categorized or classified as: "character flaws," as "biological impairments," or as "failed environmental adaptations," e.g., a person can become or learn to behave as a habitual thief; a murderer; or a liar;; or we can come face-to-face with a "biological impairment" contracted during a certain activity, accidental or deliberate, or in absence of sanitary conditions that sterilize our environment, whereby we might get diseases that may result in death, such as, in contracting AIDS; or we may be involved in an accident, such as during "bad weather," while driving a vehicle or flying a plane, due to which we might suffer harm, damage, or injuries.

According to our analysis, then, we can conclude that, first, our own "Human nature," and the "Natural environment" present certain limitations upon, not only the thoughts and ideas we might entertain so as not to get injured in some way or another, — some thoughts or ideas could be dangerous, harmful, lawless, or unjust, if executed, — but also the types of behaviors we might choose to engage in, some of which, could be fatal or deadly, e.g., jumping while inebriated, from a skyscraper, without a parachute or without some other forms of protective gear that would then prevent us from "smashing" against the building or against the ground.

Thus, we might conclude that Human nature is flawed or plagued by "sinfulness." And the Universe, or the physical-material environment of the Earth, or what we call the "natural environment," is also marred by "Entropy."

Biologically, we are "doomed to sin;" and environmentally, our transactions and relationships with the Universe are subject to Entropy.

But because our biology must also transact with the environment in ways that sustain our existence, our bodies of flesh-and-blood, are also subject to "Entropy," e.g., our lungs breathe as they extract Oxygen from

Earth atmosphere that is primarily composed of Nitrogen, Oxygen, and Hydrogen in addition to inert gases, such as Neon, and Helium, hence, "good reasons" to keep the air "as clean as possible." And that goes for the Water sources and wellsprings, as well as, for the soil comprising our natural environment or Earth ecology.

Given that we were created "from the dust of the ground of the earth," as stated in the Holy Bible; — or, given that even "Evolutionists" believe that we "emerged" from the same "cosmic soup of chemicals and elements" formed in the "Goldilock Zone" since after the so-called "big bang singularity explosion," — then, our Human Nature suffers from a combination of both "sinfulness" and "Entropy" — that we have to breathe Oxygen and we must drink clean sweet Water in order to continue to live; that we might contract fatal illnesses and diseases due to bacterial or viral infections that can result in our death; by immorally engaging in corrupt, unnatural, and abnormal sexual activities, such as sodomy and then contracting AIDS, or "Human Papilloma Virus" (HPV), accountable for some forms of deadly cancers.

Thus, "sinfulness" also "meets" or "combines with Entropy" to cause harm, damage, injury, disease, or death to Human Beings.

The very physical environment in which we live, and which we share on the Planet, contains the same cycles of repetitiveness or re-iterative patterns of flawed operations, as our own biological bodies.

Thus, these parameters, conditions, variables, circumstances, and conditions, can configure in a constellation of events or processes that can impact the ways in which we think and act, e.g., an already physiologically impaired person can experience fears and anxieties when he or she hears thunder or see lightning, that are so severe, as to result in "a heart attack;" and other events or phenomena, sum of which, can also affect the society, or "social environment" we share, e.g., a volcanic eruption can create mayhem, havoc, injuries, and extremely chaotic disruptions that can result in fomenting great emotional distress and the death of many Human Beings.

Biology is "sinful;" the Universe and the Earth, our material-physical environment, is "entropic!" And Sinfulness does, at times, "commiserate" with Entropy!

So, "Where do we go from here?" How do we get delivered from our "genetic-biological history" of travails and tribulations? How do we overcome our "spiritual being-ness" or "Human predicament," to which is attached an innate tendency or moral predisposition" to lead us astray?"

IT'S A CONTINUUM

Scriptures reveal that: "With men this is impossible; but with God all things are possible." (Matthew 19:26).

✳✳✳

LIVING WITH "ENVIRONMENTAL STRESSORS"

We're sinful in spiritual character or our "Human nature" is very flawed and error-prone. "Imagination of the thoughts of the heart:" The very distinctive quality of being able to extract abstract understanding from both our natural and social environments, — is accompanied by "weaknesses, shortcomings, flaws, and imperfections!" That is, our biological bodies also suffer from Entropy, not just "sinfulness." (Genesis 6:5; Hebrews 4:12–13.)

As we partake of the same "flawed reiterative patterns of operations," sum of which, might eventually be conducive to the termination of our existence, which we call death, both sinfulness and Entropy plague our essential capacities or potentialities, from which we inherit our capabilities to "scientifically relate," i.e., in spiritual ways that "make sense the right way" to each other and to our environments: Our own inner-self, Nature, and society, e.g., industrial pollution might endanger our sweet water supplies, sources, and wellsprings.

In fact, both sinfulness and Entropy are intrinsic to our "Human Nature," spiritually and biologically. We thrive on the Earth as "living organisms" who must transact with our physical-material environment, in ways that are so complex, that many of them remain as "mysteries" to our limited Human understanding. Hence, our common saying, "Only God knows!"

However, what we ponder continually or meditate upon for a long time, will often determine or affect the attitudes we develop about life in general; about how we relate to other people; about the content and tenor of our speech; and even about the conduct we exercise when we respond to certain situational stimuli. "Continual negative thinking" can lead to "obsessive-compulsive disorder," resulting in impairment of our ability to respond to physical or social stimuli in beneficent ways that uphold our

IT'S A CONTINUUM

health, happiness, or life. We are free indeed; but relationships are complex forms of associations that often surpass our understanding for finding a proper resolution to a certain situation, e.g., a man and a woman as a married couple, might get eventually divorced, due to what "psychologists" or "counselors" refer to as: "irreconcilable differences."

Thus, it matters what we let enter into our hearts and minds, souls and spirits. The world is full of "audio-visual stimuli," "sounds," "noises," and "events," and how we respond to them factors into ways in which we internalize attitudes and/or deduce inferences from what we experience. (Leviticus 19:17; Proverbs 4:23; 15:33; Jeremiah 4:4; 9:26; 14:9–10; Matthew 5:8, 28; 6:21; 22:37–40.)

"As a man thinketh in his heart, so is he." (Proverbs 3:26; 14:12; 29–30; 19:21; 23:6–7; 27:19).

Consequently, our "inner-life" or "mental-emotional environment," is of great importance to what pours out of our hearts when we encounter or face conditions inimical to our safety, health, or life. (Matthew 7:13–20).

By the same token, our "inner-life" or our "soul condition" or our "heart condition," can also "be a blessing" in facilitating the flow of beneficent Human relations, personal relationships, and social interactions. (Matthew 12:34–35; 22:36–40; Mark 7:14–23; Luke 6:36; 45; 11:28 12:32–34).

Our Creator, Almighty God, foreknew "our predicament," and thus, freely decided to conceive or ordain "a plan of Salvation" for our greater Human Family; a divine "plan of redemption" for Humankind, which serves to both guide us individually, and instruct us, socially. For all of us have sinned and fall short of the glory of God. (Romans 3:23; 6:23).

Enters the Word of God, for redemption, atonement, propitiation, and salvation! As prophesied through the Prophets, the Word was fulfilled by the Son of God, Christ Jesus, "the Word made flesh:" The Gospel or "the good news of Salvation" as taught and preached by His Apostles, as written, embedded, and contained in the Holy Bible! (Matthew 28:18–20; John 1:1–14).

In the same way that God said "Let there be light," Jesus said, "Father, forgive them, for they know not what they do." (Luke 23:34).

We're forgiven and that's the greatest blessing and gift from our heavenly Father through Jesus Christ our resurrected Lord and Savior.

✴✴✴

RECKONING WITH "OUR PREDICAMENT"

"The Human Condition" is: This intractable, predictable, insoluble, and unresolved contradiction plaguing our lives from birth to old age, from the diaper to the coffin!

There are many ways in which to approach "resolving" this perplexing, vexatious, paradoxical confounding "Reality" in a comprehensively, holistically, healthy manner! But God has "made a way" not only for us to "negotiate," or "navigate" through all the travails and tribulations we might encounter during our temporal earthly existence, but to also overcome all obstacles that we share with each other and our natural environment, such as our sinfulness and mortality. (John 16:32–33).

Jesus is "the way, the truth and the life." And no one comes to God but through Him! (John 14:6–7).

Every person who tries to accommodate his or her rationalizations as to "why do something" or "why to not do something," must eventually reckon with their conscience, an innate capacity for "cognitive dissonance" that might result in our choosing to do what is right in the sight of God and beneficent to one another!

But, however "situational" they might be, rationalizations only circumvent God's commandments of righteous living, so that we can "feel comfortable" in "staying where we are." Otherwise called "situational ethics," this approach to problem-solving relies on the illogical fallacy that "there are no absolutes" or that "everything is relative." "Moral relativism" or "value neutrality" is an indefensible self-delusion that has cost us, and is still costing us a lot of grief, pain, trouble, tribulation, injury, and many

IT'S A CONTINUUM

times, even death! But we breathe Oxygen to stay alive, not Carbon Monoxide! We quench our thirst naturally with sweet Water, and not Sulfuric Acid!

The flesh can resist spiritual transformation, a change of heart, or a change in worldview. But, given that our biology requires fulfillment of not only physiological needs but also emotional and social needs having connectedness with the ways in which we "associate" with "the world in which we live:" "Stasis," or "unchanging," "static processing," or "staying put," can churn for years on end, as people repeat the same patterns of thinking and the same patterns of behavior, yielding, for example, fatal drug addictions, or other forms of deadly behavioral choices.

The lure of pursuing material wealth due to pride, arrogance, fame, power, or vanity, is attached to the "patterns of thinking" and "modes of conduct" that sustain and feed those world-affirming cravings: "the lust the eyes, the lust of the flesh, and the pride of life." (1 John 2:15–17).

"This soul-condition" or "inner-spiritual dynamic" might engender a desire for satisfaction of wants rather than fulfillment of real needs, of wishes rather than actual hopes, and of inaccurate projections into the future rather than reliance upon God's will for our lives. (Proverbs 11:28; 12:17; 14:12; 29–30; 15:8–10; 19:21; Romans 8:1–11; 12:1–2).

The constellation of conditions, situations, circumstances, parameters, variables, processes, or events that we encounter during our temporary lives on the Planet, appears to be so incomprehensible and inexplicable only due to our sinful Human Nature, the depths of complexity embedded within our "socio-spiritual environment," which we call "society;" and the unfolding of "Entropy" within our biology and physical earthly environment. From either side, Human Nature and Ecological Nature, we are assailed by uncertainties that might generate anxieties and stress in our hearts and minds. But the peace of God ruling in our hearts through Christ Jesus restores certainty and security to our thought processes, situational responses, and emotions. (Colossians 3:12–17).

"Cognitive dissonance" or incompatibility between ""what is" and "what ought to be," may contrive "a sense of dislocation" or "of dissociation," between our inner-selves and the repertoire of behaviors, or the tapestry of events, unfolding before our eyes and unraveling in our lives to which we refer as "the external world."

RECKONING WITH "OUR PREDICAMENT"

As "spirit-beings," we're "only passing through" mortal existence in the material-physical Universe, during which, we have to face, to reckon with, to transact or to "deal with:" "Self, Others, and material-physical Nature!"

Each approach, perspective, worldview, or paradigm, that we attempt to "forge" to help us, guide us, direct us, or instruct us, as we endeavor to "configure" this grave sobering "Reality" apart from God's divinely ordained prescriptions for living, will eventually fail!

Human Beings contrive many "philosophical schemes" in attempts to resolve these perennial contradictions in our lives. All such "philosophical cages" end-up as "mental prisons" for their purveyors and followers whereby doctrines "revolve in a circle" without ever arriving at irrefutable or "definitive conclusions," or "box people" into stereotypes that foster prejudice, mistreatment, injustice, and cruelty.

How do we "reckon with" or "relate to" these "domains of uncertainty:" One another's Sinfulness; biological mortality; and environmental Entropy?

Resolving this conundrum, this vexing paradox, is difficult, in the short run, and persistently perplexing in the long run, because of their "intermingling alliances," or "entangling combinations." These "disheartening domains" may engender mental responses and emotional adaptations that are deleterious to peace of mind and a restful spirit.

Life and Liberty are gifts, blessings, or endowments from our Creator! Many are the choices we must make. Even more numerous are all the attempts of Human Beings at answering the greater questions that often plague our very "state of being," or "just plainly being Human!"

Where did life come from? Why is there evil in this world? Is there "an after-life" following biological death? Is there a connection between our lives on Earth and our eternal destiny in the Universe? How can we have certainty in our quest to understand these perennial paradoxes?

We are; we exist; we are real! Yet, those ultimate answers that are not yet made manifest, appear to remain beyond our capacities to grasp or acquire with complete understanding, or fulfilling comprehension! We are "in-the-know," and yet, uncertainties might cause us to have anxieties leading to stress. The only answer is: Jesus!

"In Him was life, and the life was the light of men. And the light shines in darkness; and the darkness comprehended it not." (John 1:4–5)

God had created the bright shining light of the Stars as revealed in the Book of Genesis. What is physical is physical. What is spiritual is spiritual.

IT'S A CONTINUUM

As the Apostle John teaches us through God's Holy Spirit in Christ Jesus, there is another "form of light" that is as real and true as "natural star-light."

To be "in darkness" is to be "living in sin" for which no repentance is forthcoming in the pursuit of forgiveness for newness of life. Our sinfulness contributes to the limited capacities or characteristic-capabilities of our discerning faculties.

Darkness, spiritually speaking, not only "symbolizes" the reality or presence of sinfulness and evil, amongst us and within us; but, materially darkness also "signifies" night-time darkness, or "the absence of star-light."

Cain, who murdered his brother Abel, was "in darkness;" not only had he "a sinful nature," but he succumbed to temptation; he "externalized" its imperturbable and impenetrable intrinsic dysfunctions when he killed his own brother "in cold blood." Before the coming of Christ, Humanity was permanently chained to the bondage of un-forgiven sins. Thus, Cain gave birth to "forms of behavior" that confirmed and affirmed his "need for salvation." Cain's murder of his brother also occurred before the Law, or preceding the times when God had given the Ten Commandments to Humankind through Moses.

Thus, in biblical history, from Cain to Malachi, the last Prophet under the Old Covenant preceding the birth of Christ, that is, until John the Baptist "entered the scene" by the will of God: Such was the "state of Humankind" before the coming of Christ.

Sin, inherited, not only biologically but also spiritually from Adam and Eve, was passed onto their children; which was, "the seed of rebellion" against God's sovereign authority, in imitation of Satan whom God had to cast out of Heaven for the same reasons.

As Satan sinned, in the form of a Serpent, Cain sinned, thus reflecting "the sin of rebellion" against God for which Satan was cast out of heaven by God.

In Genesis 3:15 is established the "God-ordained relationship" between "the Son of Man" and "Lucifer," "the false light," — "Cain's spiritual father" before "the Law" was established by God through Moses.

"And I will put enmity between thee and the woman, and between thy SEED and her SEED. It shall bruise thy head, and thou shalt bruise HIS heel." (Genesis 3:15).

"The seed of Satan," that is, his spirit of evil for machinations of wickedness in people who do wrong, demonstrates that those wrongdoers are

RECKONING WITH "OUR PREDICAMENT"

acting in his "image and likeness," rather than in God's own "image and likeness."

Satan exploits the sinfulness of Human Beings, which he was accountable for, in the first place, in order to "carry out" on the Earth, "the plan" that he could not bring to fruition in Heaven while he was an angel or "cherub" in service to God. That is, Satan attempted, but failed, in usurping the sovereign authority of God in the heavenly realm; but apparently, partly succeeded "in supplanting it" on Earth, in the lives of Human Beings, even before "the Law." And after "the Law," preceding the birth of Christ as well. Many times, too many to mention, God had to "discipline" the "children of Israel" for their continual rebellion against His sovereign authority, the "spirit of rebellion," "the Seed of wickedness" as propagated by Satan's hate-filled wickedness.

But God always "kept a Remnant" of faithful Israelites in order to fulfill His plan of Salvation for Humanity.

First, as a "Serpent" in Eden, Satan had deceived Adam and Eve to cause them to commit the "sin of disobedience."

But, when Christ came on the earth as "the Son of Man," while being also "the Son of the living God," Satan altered his approach or changed his plan. He "saw and opportunity and took it."

Then, Satan, figuring he'd "kill two birds with one stone," conspired to "tempt Jesus" who had sojourned in the Desert without food and water for 40 days. For Jesus was both Son of Man and Son of God. Jesus rebuked him and he went away, waiting for a "more opportune time." (Matthew 4:1–11).

Meanwhile, Satan continued to exploit the sinfulness of Humankind, as allowed by the manifestation of God's will in sinners' lives. Human Beings on the Earth, were Satan's "winning ticket" to materialize his lust for power as he continuously attempts to alter or change what would otherwise could not take place "in the heavenly realm." He failed in dethroning the Majesty of God's Omnipotence and was cast out Heaven, for once and for all.

But, Jesus had been preparing Himself for "such a time as this." Jesus, the Son of Man, was not only "fulfilling all righteousness" on Earth by submitting to being baptized by John the Baptist; but He was also commended and approved as "the Son of God" in whom "God is well pleased," stated by God, during two separate occasions. (Matthew 3:17 and 17:5; John 1:32).

Jesus had already been baptized by the Prophet John the Baptist, on the one hand, and on the other hand, God had already confirmed the

IT'S A CONTINUUM

mission of Christ on the Earth when He said, "And Jesus, when He was baptized, went up straight way out of the water; and lo, the heavens were opened unto Him, and He saw the Spirit of God descending like a dove, and lighting upon Him. And lo, a voice from heaven, saying, This is my beloved Son, in whom I am well pleased." (Matthew 3:16–17; Matthew 17:5).

But, still, Satan could not help being "utterly inane." He had to try! He cannot create anything original himself, for he, himself, was an angel, "a cherub," created by Almighty God. Satan is indeed the author of evil and the contriver of wickedness.

God's plan was a mystery, hidden, not only from Satan, but also unknown to the people whom he would use against the righteous.

And thus, as the infallible Word of God tells us in the Holy Bible:

"But we speak of the wisdom of God in a mystery, even the hidden wisdom, which God ordained before the world unto our glory, Which none of the princes of this world knew: for had they known it, they would not have crucified the Lord of Glory." (1 Corinthians 2:7–8).

A Human Person cannot simply "self-create!" And the inanimate Universe cannot simply "spew-out" the Human Mind from nothing; nor can it impart a spirit to a "living soul" which Human Beings own.

In addition, biologically speaking, there is the first Law of Bio-Genesis: That it takes "the living cells" of others, of both the Human male and the Human female, of both a Man and a Woman, as "parents," to begin our existence," to begin Human life at "fertilization," to which we refer as: "Conception!"

Were Humans to have started as "little babies" in the jungles and forests of Earth natural environment, who would have cared for them, feed and clothed them, protect them from wild animals and the elements? No adult Humans would have existed then! Thus, fails again, the theory of evolution, in providing "a godless alternative narrative" to account for the "creation" of the Universe and of Humankind in it.

The Universe was "not too bright" or "not too smart" in "creating" its own nemesis — Evolutionists believe that so-called "climate change" and "global warming" are destroying the Planet and Humans are responsible and accountable for that feat of self-destruction.

But Jesus, Son of Man and Son of God, conceived by the Holy Spirit, approved of God and to be worshipped by Human Beings as "a miracle worker" and Savior of Humanity, not only annulled and cancelled this

RECKONING WITH "OUR PREDICAMENT"

"covenant with death," but also ensured us "Continuum living" by giving us access to both "life abundant" and eternal life. (Isaiah 28:14–19).

For, Jesus, "the Emmanuel of God," means "God is with us!" (1 Corinthians 13:9–13; Revelation 22:3–5). Jesus is "the light of the world" (John 9:4–7) that casts out all anxieties sprouting from "darkness," "doubt," "blindness," and "fear;" for perfect love casts out fear. (John 9:35–41; 1 John 4:16–21).

"Then Joseph, being a just man, and not willing to make her a publick example, was minded to put her away privily. But while he thought on these things, Behold, the angel of the Lord appeared unto him in a dream, saying, Joseph, thou son of David, fear not to take unto thee Mary thy wife; for that which is conceived in her is of the Holy Ghost." (Matthew 1:19–20).

That was to fulfill the prophecy of Isaiah, the Prophet. (Isaiah 7:14; Matthew 1:23).

Jesus was both perfect Son of God and the "Seed of Woman," or, the Son of Man. In fulfillment of the Scriptures, Mary had descended from Adam and Eve, "mother of all the living," and ultimately, from the Tribe of Judah; along with Joseph, the husband of Mary, also son of Jacob his father; and of course, Jesus, who was also from the Tribe of Judah.

But Jesus was conceived by the Holy Spirit; for Mary was a virgin. (Isaiah 7:14; Matthew 1:23–25).

So, we did not exist before we were conceived in our mothers' wombs, before we were born! Where were we, then?

What constellations of events and activities "configured" in order to arrive at our present stage; to arrive in our times?

During which epoch, or age of Human living, — like "the state of the Union," so to speak, — or "State of Human Society" do we enter into existence?

At what point in "the state of Human Living" — "in the annals of Human History;" — do we receive "the gift of life?"

In which historical times, in "the History of Humans," do we encounter life, or come into being from conception to birth?

We are born into a world, during a certain period of Human History, "state of which," we know absolutely nothing!

Secular historians have divided the history of Humankind into different "ages," but apart from God's immanence and omniscience, e.g., "the stone age;" "the bronze age," etc. . .

IT'S A CONTINUUM

However, as little babies in diapers, our capacities have not yet developed to their full potentialities! Thus, we are not cognizant of our earthly condition during our time of birth.

But, historically, we, were born "in the Christian era!" For we are in the Year of our Lord; anno domini, Two Thousand and Eighteen!

Our "Reality," or "the Universe in which we live," and earthly conditions around us, began thus:

"In the beginning God created the heaven and the earth." (Genesis 1:1)

But, because we are spirit-beings created unto "the image and likeness of God," our beginnings also include the presence of God:

"In the beginning was the Word, and the Word was with God, and the Word was God." (Genesis 1:26; John 1:1).

In short, when the Holy Bible said, "Elohim," or "God" said, "Let there be light; and there was light. And the Lord God saw that the Light was good," (Genesis 1:3-4), Jesus, His Son, was also present; so was the Holy Spirit. For at the same time, — God the Father, God the Son and God the Holy Spirit, — that GOD, was creating "star-light" or "sun-light," Jesus was already "the light of the world," — that is, since before the foundation of the world:

"And the light shineth in darkness; and the darkness comprehended it not." (John 1:4-5).

God is Spirit. We have a spirit, a soul, and, a albeit mortal, biological body. Materially, and also, spiritually, God had already separated the Light from the Darkness; (Genesis 1:4), that is, God had separated Himself, from Satan, and from the material Creation He had brought into being.

Satan is "the prince of this world," whom God had cast out of Heaven; and God had also separated Himself from "the rulers of this world." (2 Corinthians 2:7-8; James 1:16-18; 4:4-8; 1 John 1:5-10).

Thus, in the same manner, God had already separated those who are His in Christ Jesus, His Seed, from the wicked people who practice evil, "the Seed of Satan." (Genesis 3:15; Matthew 25:46; Romans 8:28-30; 1 Corinthians 6:9-10; Revelation 22:14-15.)

But, says the Unbeliever: We will no longer "biologically exist" after we die! Our living existence thereby ends and our lives terminate on the Earth, in a state of "terminal Entropy" or "final Entropy," which we call, death!

RECKONING WITH "OUR PREDICAMENT"

But, still, asks the Doubter: "Where are we going?" Our "inner-being" or "inner-self" — our Soul, our Spirit, our Mind, our Heart; the "Person" within our bodies, our "decision-making free-will Self," our "Personhood," our "inner-Person,."...etc...?.

These abstract spiritual-moral "character traits of Personhood," are surely different, separate, and independent from our physical-biological bodies! The body can be "paralyzed," yet "the Mind lives!" A good example, "in our times," was Physicist Stephen Hawking! What happens to the "inner-Person" who says: "I am?"

"Where did we come from?" and "Where are we going?" make up the "conundrum" which "Human Nature" must always "deal with," even as we "wrestle" with "the Human Condition."

We, as little babies needing diapers and regular feeding from adults who gave us birth, our parents, know nothing of the world in which we find ourselves at birth. Yet, God, our Creator, foreknew us, even before we were born!

"For thou didst form my inward parts, thou didst knit me together in my mother's womb." (Psalms 139:13).

"I praise thee, for thou art fearful and wonderful. Wonderful are thy works! Thou knowest me right well; my frame was not hidden from thee, when I was being made in secret, intricately wrought in the depths of the earth. Thy eyes beheld my unformed substance; in thy book were written, every one of them, the days that were formed for me, when as yet there was none of them." (Psalms 139:15–16; Jeremiah 1:4–8; Galatians 1:15–17.)

We have "a lifespan." Laws of Thermodynamics," "Energy processing," or "Energy Transformation," demand that every thing that operates in Nature, must also have a beginning and an end. Thermodynamics thus requires "cycling of reiterative events" or of "patterns of processing," falling within the frame of "the Organizing Principle."

In short, there has to be "a method to the operations," or "modus operandi" for each phenomenon that impacts our life-support systems on the Earth.

And in durations of Time, we measure these "rates of change" or "cyclical changes" thereof, e.g., We're born; we mature and age; and then we grow old and die. Yet, we must continue to live! God blessed us with life as an indescribable gift! A blessed endowment which we are commanded to cherish and nourish in the love and admonition of the Lord! Once we accept the brevity of our existence, as a prized blessing from our Creator, we

IT'S A CONTINUUM

can then "navigate through" or "negotiate" the different cycles of repetitive events that characterize our life-span!

Don't we continuously inhale and exhale the Atmosphere into our Lungs that then extract Oxygen there-from to nourish our blood that's circulating throughout our body's organs? In the same manner, we have "sleep and wake cycles;" "labor and rest cycles;" "consumption and waste-disposal cycles."

Thus, some people might conclude that "Life is its own justification;" and hence, the reason why, that suicide and murder, are not only unthinkable, but also not committable or performable. We will die ultimately anyway; so why accelerate the process!

But as "the physical" has its own destination (Genesis 3:19); so does "the spiritual" (Luke 12:4-5). What is physical is physical; what is spiritual is spiritual (1 Corinthians 15:42-50).

Nonetheless, we choose to hope "to die only of natural causes." (Psalms 79:11; Ecclesiastes 3:2).

Some people might want to debate or open for discussion, if we choose to do so, "where we were," that is, before conception and birth. However, because we're already here, we have a life, we think and do, we ponder and act, we have a life-span, then, "where we're going" also matters.

But "Where are we going?" matters, in a way that, "Where did we come from?" cannot be framed.

For we did not know then, but, now, we do know! — that is, we didn't know "when we came into being;" or, "when we were formed" in our mother's wombs, nor when we were "created into a living being;" nor when we were born, or came out, of our mothers' wombs!

For, we did not know then; we could not have known then! But NOW, we do know that we're alive, moving, breathing, thinking, and doing! We do know! And that "makes all the difference" in the whole world, in the whole Universe! (Matthew 13:40-43; Matthew 15:17-20; Luke 6:45; John 15:22-25).

Thus, in the same manner that we are unaware of our biological-physical birth conditions, yet, the Word of God tells us: "In him we live and move and have our being" (Acts 17:22-31).

Why are they different situations, "different paradoxes," or "different conundrums?" Our ignorance at birth; and our understanding at death?

We could not self-consciously witness our own conception or birth, nor when we came out of our mothers' wombs. But, now, things are different. We are living now while fully knowing that our lives are temporary and will eventually end!

Because "we are in-the-know," because we are self-aware, (e.g., self-consciousness of good and evil, and the difference between them), and because we are aware of other Humans, — thus, we are also aware of other things, of society, of our physical environment; and of the very thoughts and ideas such knowledge and understanding generate in our hearts and minds, souls and spirits.

We are also self-conscious of such things as, the very "flawed patterns of operations" undergoing in our minds and our bodies — what we think, how our body's organs are working, and what we freely choose to do!

Even those of us who would claim "not to believe in the after-life," will entertain some form of doubting at one time or another; because the ways in which we apprehend, perceive, or understand "Reality" — or how we reckon with "Reality" (1 Corinthians 13:11–13) — through our "perceptual lenses" that often err because they rely on appearance: Our ways-and-means of apprehending Reality, limited and mortal, are also independent of the existence of that "Reality;" or disconnected from "the realness of the thing in itself" — "Der Ding an sich" (Immanuel Kant). These limited and mortal ways-and-means of apprehending "Reality," are insufficient for dismissing "Reality" as "a non-existent illusion."

But if we utilize a microscope, we might then discover the more precise ways in which things that appear, are well-ordered, according to "the Organizing Principle" that God has "embedded" within the operations of His Creation, e.g., Through "X-ray crystallography," biologists Creek and Watson were able to put together the "discovery" that our DNA has a double-helix structure.

In the same vein, as we socially relate to one another, God entreats us to "judge righteously" and not "according to appearance." (1 Samuel 16:6–7; John 7:14–24).

We have "inner-self internal consciousness" (we know that we exist; we know that we are); as well as "outer-other-self-consciousness" (we know that we are aware, that others are, or that others also exist.)

And we also possess "outer-external other-consciousness" (we know that others are aware that they also exist).

In short, (1) We know that we exist; (2) We know that we know that we exist; (3) We know that others exist; (4) And we know that we know that

IT'S A CONTINUUM

others do exist; (5) And we know that we know that others also know that we do exist and that they also exist!

That means, whether or not there is indeed "an after-life," its existence is independent of "our belief systems." God does not seek His own interest; for He is self-sufficient! But we are not! We are "created beings:" We have a beginning, a life-span, and an end! We exist "from the diaper," until comes, our time "for the coffin."

And given that we can know, and do know, that we can neither verify its existence, nor confirm its non-existence: Then, we have to take God's Word seriously concerning this matter! No one can die and return to life to tell us whether "the after-life" exists or not!

Our "belief systems," e.g., "Existentialism;" or "thought systems," e.g., "Marxian Dialectics," "Epiphenomenalism," etc. . .., are irrelevant to the true authentic existence of that "after-life Reality." We will be "long gone" before the discussion ends. (Matthew 18:7 Luke 11:28; John 9:39–41).

The group of believers called "Existentialists," will answer those questions by saying that: No mortal Human Being can prove that there is no "after-life!" That's called "a double negative" or that "we cannot disprove there is no after-life."

But, before we were conceived and born, we did not exist; and after we die, we will no longer exist. We're conceived to be born, to live, and then to die! "Point final!" And that's that! Period! Though these supposed assurances will be uttered by "Scientists," — or people who believe that only the material-physical Universe which we can "handle with our biological senses" is real, — but such pretenses of certainty without valid reproducible proof are, "not scientific." For, a principle of the Scientific Method is that experimental results must be reproducible for verification by independent, disinterested, and unbiased researchers.

Jesus Christ rose from the dead and ascended unto Heaven, after which He empowered us with the knowledge of His Holy Spirit, to ensure and seal the Reality of our "spiritual existence" in the "world to come" (the "New heaven and new earth"); or in the "after-life" (going to Heaven or ending-up in Hell!) (Isaiah 65:17; 66:1; 22; Matthew 25:40–46; Mark 13:1–2; Luke 17:37; 1 Corinthians 15:42–58).

However, the same "Existentialist" who rejects God's existence; who denies the existence of our spirit and soul; who dismisses the Reality of our "inner-self" as being independent of our biology; and who objects to "the Realness" of the abstract Mind we possess that allows us to think and form ideas: He or she, that so-called "Existentialist," will still cling to "the abstract rules, regulations, laws, or statutes" that govern, instruct, or inform our knowledge of the sanctity of his or her inalienable right "to possess or own property;" he or she will demand respect for his or her Human dignity, —abstract non-physical spiritual concepts — when confronted with every or any attempt at violating his or her "Human rights" or "civil rights;" he or she will expect, desire, or demand "justice be done" in cases before a court of law, so that the decision is either in his or her favor, or against his or her disadvantage.

How do we "reconcile" such baffling contradictions! These contradictions are, to say the least, "mind-boggling." Hence, this perplexing, vexatious, and confounding paradox: "Human nature" engaged in "navigating" through, or "negotiating," our "Human condition!"

Existentialists will use an abstraction that he or she does not believe in, e.g., a mental spiritual construct called "a Law," so as to justify or rationalize his or her "right" to possessing or owning property, which is a concrete physical thing.

But did not God say, "Let there be light and then there was light!" Then, is it not the Spirit who brings things into existence? (Isaiah 48:12–13; Romans 4:16–18; 1 Corinthians 1:28–31; Hebrews 11:1–3).

Some "Existentialists" will not deny that Human Beings have a "real Mind," but will declare it to be "an emergent property of our brain;" and/or they will hold that, when the brain dies, so does the abstract Mind; the Soul; the inner-self; the spirit or "the Heart!"

To "Existentialists," only "the physical" or what can be perceived through our biological senses is "real." Thus, given that we can hold an apple in our hands, we should also be able to "handle" or "hold our Minds" in our hands! However, "Existentialists" will hold that even if an abstraction is real, then, it must be "an emergent property of the Human brain:" meaning that, self-consciousness arose from the modus operandi of the brain itself, but has no independent existence or Reality. The brain dies; so does self-consciousness.

But, as God's Word elucidates this matter: That which is physical is physical; and what is abstract-spiritual is spiritual. (Romans 8:5–11; 10:1–4; 1 Corinthians 2:6–16).

But, even if we cannot produce, nor handle, nor hold the very Mind that "Existentialists" will admit to be real, and which they are utilizing in marshalling an argument against the facticity of the real existence of the

IT'S A CONTINUUM

Human Mind, then, their own Minds are indeed the fundamental proofs that, though the Human Mind is not "physical," it is "truly Real."

And given that "living in the Reality of our Human Existence" in all its encompassing breadth and scope, is our meaningful purpose, then, objectively speaking, God who is Creator of all things is also the transcendent author of our abstract Minds.

"Existentialists" will also deny the Reality of moral principles that guide Human thinking, and inform and instruct Human actions, i.e., good and evil; right and wrong, but will also clamor for "informed consent," which is an abstract principle governing the biological behavior of Human Beings, sum of which, intricately and intrinsically connected with the free will exercise of our God-given Liberty.

And that perplexing contradictory "paradoxical attitude" will correspond to the ways in which Existentialists want to "frame circumstances," events and conditions affecting their living existence! They will recognize that some things are "good," and that other things are "bad," even from the simple standpoint of the "pain and pleasure principle," e.g., Given that they deny that there is Sinfulness in our Human nature; and given that there is Lawfulness as ordained by our Creator, then, Existentialists might "see nothing wrong" with "legalizing" all illicit drugs based upon their belief in "freedom without limits," or "liberty without boundaries," in spite of the very laws that they know, protect their very lives and property, and against which, of course, they surely do not protest.

And it is through such confounding paradoxes engendering only confusion and disorder in the Human Mind, that the Devil takes opportunity "to work through Human sinful nature," for establishing activities in our society, such as infanticide by abortion; or hedonism in the guise of "free love" masquerading as sodomy and lesbianism.

Thus, Spiritual matters are deemed "abstractions," by Existentialists, or as an "emergent property of our Biological Brain," such that, even though, those very same abstract spiritual principles will govern, not only Human sentiments and attitudes, but also, the course of their choices of behavior, conduct, actions, and activities. (John 8:39–47).

Did not the Pharisees on the Sanhedrin and the High Priest "orchestrate" the provocations and incitements that gave rise to "the mob rule" clamoring that Jesus be crucified and that Barabbas, the robber and murderer, be released? (Luke 23:13–25; John 18:37–40; 19:7–11).

RECKONING WITH "OUR PREDICAMENT"

In short, there is always "room for improvement," especially of this, "our Human condition." For certain abstract realities, such as the very facticity of the existence and operations of our Minds; the capacity to remember our dreams or analyze our past errors for corrections and amendments; and the very ability to "intuitively infer" and "logically deduce" their meaning for purposes of present existence or for "life in the future," are utterly undeniable and irrefutable that such abstract spiritual principles are "Realities," albeit, which, we cannot yet fathom, understand, or explain, and consequently, which, we call: "Mysteries of the Universe."

Some processing routines for mental functions appear to share a certain familiarity with the thermodynamic mechanism, Input-Process-Output. For example, we learn moral values that then direct our obedience to certain "rules of civilization," such as, our "rights to own and dispose of our own property."

Yes, there might be "apparently similar encapsulations" in Nature or scientific applications, of the patterns of information processing that are peculiar to the Human Brain.

But, that certain frequencies and wavelengths in the electro-magnetic radiation spectrum will: "carry information," — as in a "compact Disk or CD," or "a movie projector," — does not make the CD or projector, "an intelligent self-conscious robot" having free will. For, "self-determination," is purely a Human characteristic or "spiritual endowment."

Comparing the ways in which our Minds can "record information," or "remember events," — via brain-centered senses that are "activated" by nerves with cells or "neurons" having synaptic clefts, through which, are traveling, "electro-chemical impulses" that are believed to be "carrying music" to our ear drums for our understanding and enjoyment, e.g., while playing a "music CD," — to the ways in which mechanical contraptions we invent or "robotic functionalities" that we design to operate also via "electro-magnetic radiation energy"— also "carrying information" through wires connected to transistors and microchips, whereas in Human Beings electro-chemical impulses flow from neurons to neurons — still, cannot justify our establishing "identical similarity" between the two activities, the first, "biological self-conscious spiritual understanding;" and the second, "electro-chemical binary encoding" of microchips for generating mechanically produced outputs that, albeit, accomplish specific tasks, e.g., printing a report; or detecting oil deposits beneath the surface of the Earth below the Oceans.

IT'S A CONTINUUM

The two processes are "not identical," though they — the Human Brain and the "music CD" or "printing machine" — might display "some similarities" that inhere in the Form of "information processing activities" being performed by both the Brain and the music CD or the printing machine; however, inanimate "information processing" is a "mechanical Form" as opposed to a "self-aware Spiritual Form" that is different in kind and degree from the "binary encoding Form" espoused by the music CD or printing machine.

Therefore, mechanical "recording of information," and "binary processing of information" for task performance or production of outputs, absent the quality of Self-consciousness for free will choice-making, cannot be declared "identical" to spiritual physiological-biological self-aware ways-and-means of acquiring and utilizing abstract knowledge and understanding. Machines are not Human; and Humans are "spirit-beings."

Self-conscious intelligence does not arise, "spontaneously," from inanimate Matter. And to say that it is "an emergent property of the Human Brain" does not explain cause-and-effect operations accountable for its origin, nor does it give details of the way it had "emerged;" or of how it was "created." After all, a "pebble-stone" does not "think;" it's simply there!

Can an inanimate Universe "create" Human Self-Conscious Spiritual Intelligence with innate capabilities to design, invent, and manufacture "robotic machines" that can then destroy the Earth through nuclear bombs technologies? Is the Universe "suicidal" then?

Evolutionism is a self-destructive suicidal machine-oriented and technology-directed worldview that is not only illogical and unscientific, but also unfit for Human belief or abstract Human faith.

The Human Brain yields Self-consciousness and freedom of volition, which the music CD or the printing machine can never have.

Self-iterative patterns of information processing via circulation or currency of electro-chemical impulses, are present in both instances; but their structure, organization, function, operations, and purpose are intrinsically and meaningfully different. They are not "self-identical."

Self-aware capabilities of ideas formation, intuition, discernment, or thinking processes, or of "creating Meaning," are not qualities or characteristics found in a "music CD" or a "printing machine." Machines can be "programmed" to mimic Human capabilities; but that's not the equivalent of self-determined freedom of volition.

RECKONING WITH "OUR PREDICAMENT"

For example, a CD or "compact disk" can "record music," because when it is manufactured it is "programmed" to "record music;" but the "music CD can never know "that it knows, that it knows," it's "recording music." It is an inanimate machine that has neither Self-consciousness nor free will for independent choice-making decisions.

Therefore, similarity of Form, e.g., "Recording of information," or "processing of information," alone, does not give the "music CD" or "printing machine," a "self-conscious Mind" or a "self-aware Consciousness!"

The Form in methods of information retention and processing may share some similarities in their "operational mechanics" or "modus operandi;" however, these self-iterative patterns of information recording and processing for producing certain outputs, respectively, are not "self-identical."

Thus, only we, do, have an invisible but truly REAL SELF-CONSCIOUS MIND HAVING SELF-AWARENESS OF FREE WILL FOR INDEPENDENT CHOICE-MAKING DECISIONS! Not the machines we invent or technologies we create to assuage the burdens of our daily labors!

Both Water and Sulfuric Acid are "liquids;" but the one is a life-sustaining fluid, whereas the other is a toxic poison for the Human Organism.

Does not The Holy Bible even tell us, that as "children of God" who are "born of the Spirit" in Jesus Christ, our Lord and Savior, we do "have the Mind of Christ?" (1 Corinthians 2:14–16). Yes, the Word of God is true, for "God is not a man that He should lie." (Numbers 23:19).

Though we are conceived and born to live and then to die while having to reckon with the vexatious perplexity of all the paradoxes that afflict our sentiments and attitudes towards our own selves, towards other people, towards the things we own due to their utility, and towards the undeniable reality of the abstractness of our Minds, Emotions, and Will, the Holy Bible tells us that we are "created a little less than God." (Psalms 8: 3–8).

The albeit "flawed operations" of our abstract Mind, can be made manifest in how they affect physiological processes of our biological body; or can convict us or persuade us to commit certain actions having either good or bad consequences for self, others, society, and the natural environment. And we do know that — but the "music CD" or "the printer-robot" can never know that! (Proverbs 14:12; 15:22; 16:7, 25; 19:21).

Human Beings have the powerful capacity to "plan an activity," e.g., a wedding. The machine, however, must be programmed with instructions or inputs that it processes, in order to produce outputs. We have God-given Liberty from which we enjoy many freedoms in accordance with "just powers from the consent of the governed." (Declaration of Independence of the United States of America, 1776 AD).

The Constitution of the United States begins with "We the People of the United States." And not we the robots; nor we the machines; nor we the computers! Humans have free will; but machines, in whatever form, do not! The Constitution is written for People, and not for machines, not for robots, and not for lower animal life-forms.

God decided to give us a way out of this vexatious, perplexing, confounding, complex, unfathomable, inexplicable, and incomprehensible paradox: "His plan of Salvation!"

✱✱✱

WHY WE NEED TO BE "SAVED?"

THERE ARE NATURAL DISASTERS such as tornadoes, earthquakes, volcanic eruptions, and hurricanes; there are unpredictable accidents due to mechanical failure or human error while driving an automobile; and there are even certain birth defects and other pre-natal anomalies, such as "Down's Syndrome" that appears to have no physiological cause or biological explanation, except that physicians might call them "errors of gene replication" due to abnormalities in either RNA processing or DNA operations.

We are born as little babies; as little infants who need diapers, special feeding at regular intervals, by our mothers' breast milk, and whose every need is broadcast by some kinds of "baby cries." (Proverbs 20:24).

We have capacities to learn to think and speak, which later develop into capabilities, to read and write.

But how does a little baby in diapers who can't even feed himself or herself acquire their worldview, belief system, faith, or perspective, to then, become so arrogant, as to be boastful, vain, corrupt, lawless, or abusive?

What happens "between the diaper and the coffin" appears to be "an insoluble puzzle" needing "a Designer" to put it together.

Such a "vexing paradox," remains one of the greatest mysteries of Human living. Socio-biologists would say that "it's 50 % genetics and 50 % environment."

In short, none of us really knows all the factors that account for "how a person turns out" in life. Hence, the saying, "Time will tell!"

As we are developing and growing up, we learn from many sources of information and wellsprings of knowledge. Information might be transient, or based on contextual situations having unknown conditions and variables; but knowledge has a greater validity due to certainty in its veracity, e.g., death comes to us all, eventually.

IT'S A CONTINUUM

Additionally, we absorb certain "forms of thinking," sources of which, we do not care to analyze, know, understand, or fathom at a deeper level, e.g., things we learn from our parents, teachers, or peers.

Our Minds also generate new ideas from observations of events and analyses of processes, natural and social, that we encounter as we temporarily journey upon the Earth, including "other things" we learn "along the way," through "intuitive apprehension" or "spiritual discernment."

However, we already know that we have "a Sinful Nature" embedded within "an Entropic environment," entanglements of which, accountable for "the Human Condition."

We are flawed not only in activities of observations but also in activities of analyses. Thus, even abstractions that our biological brain might extract from external observations or internal pondering might not necessarily be accurate. And hence, our continual need for compassionate corrections and loving admonitions.

The problem is really, not "how to be good," but rather, "how to thwart evil;" how to avert wickedness; how to prevent accidents; or how to prepare for anticipated "natural disasters."

Human Nature does not need any "training" in selfishness and wickedness. But we do need lots of help in how to be righteous and just on the Earth with our fellow Human Beings.

Some patterns of thinking and forms of behavior, we can "manage," "master," "subdue" or "overcome," through temperance and self-control; but, due to our sinful nature and Entropy, there are others that are said to be "more visceral," and thus, more difficult to overcome, such as getting angry much too often; exercising the will to freely repent; letting go of hatred based on external appearance; generalizing people's cultural habits into "a well-packaged stereotype;" abandon prejudicial biases against learnt stereotypes; and/or foregoing violence as a means of conflict resolution.

Still, we must live, "have a life," "survive," "thrive," and "prosper," as we endeavor to "carve our destiny" on this Planet, in accordance with the Lord's Will, "until death do us part." But God does not want us to simply "manage evil," but rather, to "overcome evil with good." (Romans 12:18–21.)

Therefore, the only question that remains to be addressed is: How are we to live? Oftentimes, it is "feelings" that control attitudes and sentiments held regarding certain things in life, rather than spiritual principles or moral precepts. Regrettably, a lot of people tend to "look at things" the way they "feel about them." But "feelings" are often transient, inaccurate,

WHY WE NEED TO BE "SAVED?"

inappropriate, wrong, bad, and even toxic to our mental health, spiritual maturity, and emotional intelligence.

The ways we think and act, speak and move on the Earth do impact our heavenly destiny, as we live out, or practice our faith in God.

"For as the body apart from the spirit is dead, so faith apart from works is dead." (James 2:26).

And because we are "spirit-beings" intrinsically having innate needs for moral guidance in the ways we think and do, we are also "social beings" who inherently need love, friendship, fellowship, companionship, and association with other Human Beings. Then, the ultimate question becomes: How ought we to live in our relationships with other mortal Humans like us in society? What kinds of attitudes and sentiments should we hold regarding our earthly environment? Is it one of "stewardship" or "conquest?"

Where is the best source of knowledge or original wellspring of spiritual principles for righteous moral living?

Where do we obtain the fundamental basics for "thinking right" and "acting right," or for the kinds of thinking and ideas formation that we need in order to "live as we ought?" To give glory to God through our works of righteous faith, and to magnify the name of Jesus in all we undertake with the help of the Holy Spirit; in short, to "do the Truth in love!" (Ephesians 4:15).

"Have nothing to do with godless and silly myths. Train yourself in godliness; for while bodily training is of some value: but godliness is of value in every way, as it holds promise for the present life and also for the life to come." (2 Timothy 4:7–8).

Nature, or our physical earthly environment, cannot "talk to us" in comprehensible speech; neither can lower forms of life, such as "animals" — only other Human Beings can.

But, at certain times, we can always freely describe our contentment in enjoying the beauty of "natural scenery!" But we cannot "worship the created" instead of the Creator. (Romans 1:16–23.)

There are ways to "appreciate Nature" that glorify the Creator, rather than "the creature," e.g., Poets and other writers will sometimes "romanticize" a sunrise, a sunset, lightning, thunder, a mountain, a forest, or a flower, in an artistic manner derived from what we've been taught to appreciate and value; and will interpret other things as they've learned to discard and dismiss them, e.g., lightning and thunder; rain and snow etc. . .

IT'S A CONTINUUM

But Scriptures tell us that the whole Creation "declares" God's glory in both their workings and functionalities.

"The heavens declares the glory of God; and the firmament shows his handy-work; Day unto day utter speech, and night unto night show knowledge. There is no speech nor language where their voice is not heard." (Psalms 19:1–3).

In short, God's glory is self-evident in His wondrous and mysterious Creation!

In sum, as spirit-beings created "in the image and likeness of God," we can't escape from spiritual reasoning, valuated analyses, and moral actions! The spiritual-moral dimension in our lives is therefore inescapable. We know the difference between good and evil, and between right and wrong, and God's commandments to pursue the good, seek peace, and do what is right in His sight. (Micah 6:8).

The inner-faculties we possess can be described as "spiritual-scientific." Mental functions and intuitive apprehensions from "information processing" can yield "self-awareness knowledge" and self-conscious understanding. "And God said Let there be light, and there was light." (Genesis 1:3).

As Darkness flees in the presence of Light, ignorance dissipates in the presence of knowledge; and the Good flourishes by displacing evil and neutralizing its destructive consequences through wisdom and understanding. However, labeled or called, e.g., good or evil; good or bad, right or wrong, deciding on these spiritual principles for the pursuit of righteousness, has been imparted to us, so as "to guard" our hearts and minds, "with all diligence," for from them, flow "the springs of life." (Proverbs 4:23; John 7:37–39; 1 Timothy 6:20–21).

Human Beings do know and do desire what they perceive or consider to be "good," "advantageous" or "beneficial;" in the same vein, they will tend to shun those things that they hold to be deleterious, dangerous, or destructive to their well-being, e.g., given a choice, we'd rather be richer than poorer; ride in a vehicle to cover long distances rather than simply walking; keeping our hands safely "tucked away" from a hot stove burner.

Thus, because we have this innate need to pursue our own interests, Human Beings, must have spiritual instruction and moral guidance to direct "our path in life" — yes, from little "babies in diapers" to the time when we'll "need a coffin;" that is, from infancy through mature adulthood, until "we pass away."

WHY WE NEED TO BE "SAVED?"

And that will never change! But it is often said, "with age comes wisdom!" Hopefully, godly wisdom! (Psalms 4:4-6; Proverbs 1:7; 8:10-14; 1 Corinthians 2:3-7).

"What we preach is not ourselves, but Jesus Christ as Lord, with ourselves as your servants for Jesus' sake. For it is the God who said, Let light shine out of darkness, who has shone in our hearts to give the light of the knowledge of the glory of God in the face of Christ. But we have this treasure in earthen vessels, to show that the transcendent power belongs to God and not to us." (2 Corinthians 4:5-7).

Selfish greed, vain arrogance, and prideful covetousness corrode the very depths of the Human soul. They gnaw at our inner-being for transmogrifying our healthy spiritual intelligence into "emotional weapons" that can wreck havoc in our neighbors' lives.

Because of our Human frailties due to both Sinfulness and Entropy, we always need to depend upon God "to work out our salvation, with fear and trembling," through pursuing not only our own interests but also through caring about "our neighbor's interests" as well, for the fulfillment of our all innate needs. (1 Corinthians 14:12; 1 Corinthians 16:13; 2 Corinthians 5:14-15; 12:19; Galatians 5:13-15; Philippians 2:1-11).

Preachers, teachers, pastors, and ministers of God's Word love us, teach us, pray for us, preach to us, and admonish us towards being more "Christ-like;" Farmers grow food; truck drivers, train conductors, and ship's captains labor to transport our food where it needs to be, whether in warehouses or stores; nurses and physicians attend to our medical needs and mental health; gas station attendants supply our provisions to obtain fuel for our vehicles; construction workers or civil engineers build our homes, buildings, houses, industries, roads, or churches; instructors are trained to teach in classrooms nested in buildings called "schools," "colleges," "academies," or "universities."

In sum, we don't live "in a jungle" where "anything goes," notwithstanding what Evolutionists believe! Humanity would not have survived up to today by living in a lawless, disorganized, unstructured, disorderly, random, accidental manner. For the "Organizing Principle" requires continuous prudence, training, watchfulness, understanding, and stewardship. (Psalms 19:14; 34:11-14; 37:1-4; 53:1).

"Except the Lord build the house, they labor in vain that build it; except the Lord keep the city, the watchman waketh but in vain." (Psalms 127:1-2).

IT'S A CONTINUUM

The house of which the Psalmist is speaking is "God's holy habitation," God's temple, which, through Christ we have become, transformed into "a work of righteousness" with Jesus "at the helm, drafting our journey" throughout our lives. Lest we "be tossed to and fro and carried about with every wind of doctrine." (1 Corinthians 3:9; 16; 2 Corinthians 5:1–5; 6:14–18; Galatians 3:6–7; Ephesians 1:9–10; 4:11–16).

An organized order structured as "a System," necessarily requires careful and prudent planning, mapped direction, meaningful functions, and blue-printed purpose.

We are socially attuned Spirit-beings with a soul comprising our thoughts, emotions, and free will; and both thought and experience teach us, through spiritual principles of good and evil, and of right and wrong, that "we need each other!" As it is often said, "Humans are social by nature."

For example, apart from sunrise and sunset, birds naturally flying, and butterflies frolicking amongst flowers: As above intimated, every thing that happens to a Human Being living and sharing in our society, originates from another Human Being, from having food to eat to being involved in an automobile accident, especially in such a highly technologically developed society as ours.

It is people who labor and work "to make things work" how they ought to. It is people who diligently labor to make things work well-and-right as they should. Likewise, barring a fatal attack from a wild untamed animal, earthquakes, volcanic eruptions, tornadoes and storms, or some other forms of meteorological phenomena: Evil, wrongs, transgressions, iniquities, injuries, and trespasses also originate from other mortal Humans like us.

How ought we to live as we reckon with "the Realities" constituting "our social inter-dependence?"

"People need people!" Yes, but it is our faith in God through the Holy Spirit of Christ Jesus, that makes the difference in "how we treat each other;" even as we are entreated and admonished to bear one another's burdens. (Matthew 5:1–16; 33–35; 6:14; 19–20; 7:12–14; 9:36–38; Philippians 1:9–11; 2:12–13).

"Do unto others as you would have them do unto you. For this sums up the Law and the Prophets." (Matthew 7:12).

Remember: We come into this world as little babies in diapers who must be continuously cared for and attended to, until such a time we grow up, and mature enough to obtain a certain amount of knowledge, level of understanding, and degree of self-regulation, so that we can then transact and relate with each other in society, peacefully, justly, and lawfully, as we overcome all obstacles that might impair our mutual welfare, by "doing the Truth in love!" (1 Corinthians 13:1–13; 2 Corinthians 13:8–10; Philippians 3:16.)

Not one of us is "born already knowing!" And life itself is a rich field of experiences from which we continue to learn during "all the living we're making." We spend roughly a quarter of our life-span "in a school environment" in order to learn not only the "rules of civilization," but, hopefully, also the ultimate sovereign authority of God in the unfolding of Human history. (Proverbs 22:6; Isaiah 28:9–10; 13; Romans 1:16–32).

Thus, we learn from each other, from events we experience, from reading and learning from God's Word; and from our own "spiritual-reasoning activities" proceeding from our souls, i.e., intellect, emotions, and free will, sum of which, yielding or climaxing into certain conclusions, inferences, and deductions that we decide to "adopt as components of our faith in God." For example, the Holy Bible does not specifically address "how to drive a car" or "how to react" to another driver's undisciplined conduct, but experience has taught us that "courtesy is always a good policy."

In professional parlance, or fields of academia, these are referred to as: "Thought systems" acquired via "The Cognitive Domain," (the intellect); "the Affective Domain," (feelings, emotions, attitudes etc. . .); and "the Psycho-Motor Domain" (how we learn to do as we've been taught).

We are predisposed both "to spiritually reason," and genetically, to "believe in a certain worldview," or "to have a philosophy of life!" (Isaiah 1:18–20; 43:25–28; 1 Corinthians 6:1–3; 8:1–6; Galatians 3:8–19; Ephesians 4:17–24; Colossians 2:6–15; 2 Thessalonians 3:13; 1 Timothy 4:7–10; Hebrews 8:13;13:8; 1 Peter 4:6–10).

Remember: God said "Let there be light; and there was light; and the Lord saw that the light was good: And God divided the Light from the Darkness." (Genesis 1:3–4).

"Belief systems" can be "light" or they can be "darkness." "Works of darkness" symbolize "evil works;" whereas, "children of light" believe and practice the Truth as God has declared it to be, for love, liberty, compassion, charity, equality, justice, and lawfulness, as we seek the good, pursue peace, and do justly while walking humbly before the Lord. (Micah 6:8; John 12:36; 14:15–17; Romans 6:4; 12:21; 1 Corinthians 14:20; 2 Corinthians 4:6; Galatians 5:5–7; Ephesians 5:6–15; Colossians 1:11–14.)

IT'S A CONTINUUM

Even those who pretend not to have "a belief system," in adhering to "unbelief," as a worldview, are subscribing to a "thought system" or "belief system," which, when applied to all things in their lives, can be said to have become "a religious faith:" That of "atheism," or of "secular humanism." (That is, Humans, taken "to have worth," or considered "to have value," apart from God' sovereign powers of Creation). "Humanists" evaluate all things within a framework of appraisal that "totally takes God out of the picture."

"You believe there is only one God; you do well. Even the devils believe and shudder" (Deuteronomy 6:4–9; James 2:19).

But we can't merely believe in just "any thing that comes along." Oft repeated is the adage: "He who does not believe in something will fall for anything." Hence, why God has decided to impart to us, capacities or giftedness to have Faith, to labor in Love, and to live with Hope.

"So faith, hope, love abide, these three; But the greatest of these is love." (1 Corinthians 13:13).

The infallible and inerrant Word of God tells us:

"Faith is the substance of things hoped for and the evidence of things not seen. For by it the elders obtained a good report. Through faith we understand that the worlds were framed by the Word of God, so that things which are seen were not made of things which do appear." (Hebrews 11:1–3).

Thus, what we believe in our heart of hearts, or adopt as our Faith, does matter so much, that it concerns whether we live or die. Think about it. What would happen if every Person in society was a thief, a robber, a murderer, and a liar?

That's the whole and only purpose for our Creator to have imparted Faith to our inner-being so that our good works, consistent with that righteous faith, overflow in the world, even as we glorify God by our loving acts towards each other, especially towards those in the household of God. (2 Corinthians 13:8–9; Galatians 3:19; Ephesians 4:30–32).

Faith in God gives us great Hope in the present, for peace and assurance in situations that confront our abilities to remain free from bondage, and certainty for the future, which for the most part we cannot forecast. (Micah 6:8; Jeremiah 29:11, KJV; John 3:16; John 17:3).

However, we can believe God's prophecies because His Word never returns void but accomplishes the purpose for which it is sent. (Isaiah 14:24; 31:2; 40:28–31 42:6–9; 43:10–13; 46:10–11).

WHY WE NEED TO BE "SAVED?"

And that's why we are entreated by God's Word to "walk by faith, not by sight." (2 Corinthians 5:70).

For God's promises are "yeah and Amen." (Romans 14:19; 1 Corinthians 12:12–13; 2 Corinthians 1:20–22; Ephesians 1:13–14; 1 Thessalonians 5:15:21; 2 Thessalonians 3:13).

Christ has taken our punishment by dying on the Cross; thereafter, He was buried; but He rose from the dead to seal the Kingdom of God in us as His inheritance. (2 Corinthians 1:20–22; 2 Peter 1:5–11).

"While you have the light, believe in the light, that you may become sons of light." (John 12: 36.)

For, "Jesus Christ is the same, yesterday, today and forever." (John 12:34; Hebrews 13:8).

The Holy Spirit seals us as "heirs with Christ," in the kingdom of God. Thus, we no longer stand condemned, but sanctified as faithful doers of righteous works, as directed and guided by God's Holy Spirit indwelling our hearts (Romans 8:1–11; 2 Corinthians 1:20–22; Ephesians 1:11–14).

Thus, because of this great assured Hope, our love for one another can be genuine, sincere, and honest; meaning, that we can love each other "without dissimulation," "evasion" or "mental reservation." (Romans 12:9; 1 Corinthians 13:4–6; 2 Corinthians 4:1–2).

"Human Nature" is more complex than mere hormonal-physiological processes and binary operations transmitted via nerves activated by electrolytic chemical stimuli. For God in Christ Jesus by His Holy Spirit can make all things NEW, so that, not only are we capable of transcending or overcoming our "Human Nature," but also that we can henceforth strive to prosper in our living, even as God's representatives on the Earth! (Isaiah 42:6–9; 43:18–19; 48:6; 62:2; 66:22; Romans 12:1–2; 2 Corinthians 5:14–17).

We possess an abstract Mind that we cannot handle, grasp or hold in our hands! Our faculties perform such awesome creative feats of discovery, that it is sometimes called "the sixth sense," "intuition," or "discernment," depending on the context within which the activity or event takes place.

Lower life forms or animals, cannot reflect upon their condition; nor can they change their Species-specific genetic imprinting. Human Beings help each other and depend on each other for fulfilling certain innate needs.

Yet, we don't have an innate need for tobacco, alcohol, or illicit drugs; nor for an habitual addiction to other things, such that might defraud, devalue, demean, and degrade the character-qualities of God, which He had,

IT'S A CONTINUUM

not only imparted to us since before the time of Creation, but also that we have obtained through spiritual rebirth in the love of Christ Jesus whose precious blood cleanses us from all unrighteousness. (1 John 1:8-10).

But, given that we all suffer from the same flawed "Human Nature," i.e., sinfulness; and given that our very biological organism is subject to environmental, and internal physiological Entropy, none of us can "save each other!" Nor can we "save ourselves!" (Genesis 21:12; 22:7-14; Exodus 17:3-7; Leviticus 19:1-2; 12:44; 17:11; 20:26; Deuteronomy 18:18-22; Isaiah 12:10-13; 65:18; 66:1-4; Romans 9:7-8; Hebrews 11:18).

And that's why, as John 3:16 proclaims, God had to send Christ Jesus in the form of a man, to take our place on the Cross, rise from the dead, and ascend unto Heaven, so as to empower us with His risen Holy Spirit for "life more abundant," and eternal life. (John 17:3; 1 John 2:21-25).

Thus, "from the diaper to the coffin," — forgive us for underlining these verities so often; but they help us "keep things in perspective" — though uniquely distinct individual Persons, albeit mortal, we, Human Beings, remain indubitably social, needful, and dependent upon each other in ways that still allow us to enjoy our freedoms the Liberty for which Christ has set us free. (Galatians 5:1; 13).

Even as adults, we need and obtain love and compassion from each other, as much as we obtain "services" in the forms of purchases or sales, nursing care, or funeral services, from one another.

From "Human Services" to "Home-Health Services:" God has structured our world so that, as we rely upon His loving kindness for our wellbeing, we are also sharing our common destiny as "children of God," in being "forgiven builders" of His kingdom on the Earth.

We need God's presence — the greatest of all "deliverance services" that is "free of charge," for we are "saved by grace." (Ephesians 2:8-10).

Through Christ's Holy Spirit, God's care for us alleviates our burdens and lightens our loads, in a world where Sinfulness and Entropy govern both biological processes and ecological phenomena. (Matthew 11:28-30; 1 Thessalonians 5:9-11; 2 Timothy 2:6-10).

For it is "Christ in us, the Hope of glory" whose sacrificial love, compassionate forbearance, and empowering Spirit, who gives us our Faith that is "the victory that overcomes the world." (Galatians 5:5-6; Colossians 1:27-29; 1 Thessalonians 2:10-12; 5:15-24; 1 John 5:4-5).

Why does our Faith "overcome the world?" Because "perfect love casts out fear;" for there is no fear in love; fear has to do with punishment;

WHY WE NEED TO BE "SAVED?"

but we stand no longer condemned, but forgiven, sanctified, justified, and ultimately, glorified with Christ when He does return! (Romans 8:1–11; Romans 12:1–2; 1 John 4:17–19). More than that, Jesus tells us not to look for God's Kingdom as something to be "located" at a certain place or in a certain geographical area. We are "spiritual carriers" of God's Kingdom in this Universe!

"The Kingdom of God is within you." (Luke 17:20–21; 2 Corinthians 2:17; Colossians 4:19).

The Spirit of God in us enlightens our hearts for living in this world. And "How we ought to live," is, in summary, dependent upon what's being "processed" within our inner-being, contained in our souls, or dependent upon "who indwells our hearts," e.g., "how we think," "how we feel," "how we see or understand," "how we perceive each other," "the worldview that animates our ideas and actions," etc. . ., even as we transact within our social world and our earthly environment, e.g., "how we relate to each other" regarding the utilization of resources with which God has already blessed us, by embedding every thing that we'll ever need for "living well," within the very Creation he brought into being for our sakes, while, through sending Christ Jesus as our Redeemer, Lord, and Savior, in order to "destroy the works of the devil" at the same time.

By the rebirth of our spirit, as affirmed "through baptism" in the name of the Father, the Son and the Holy Spirit, we obtain confirmed forgiveness and provable newness of life. (Isaiah 59:20; Matthew 15:8–9; Mark 7:10–23; 2 Corinthians 3:4–6; 1 John 3:7–10).

And where is the best original infallible Source but from our omniscient, omnipresent, loving heavenly Creator Almighty God: He has "the original blueprint" for "our essential being-ness," for who we are, as Human Beings — "the very thing in itself!" as the author Immanuel Kant, has put it: "Der ding an sich!" (James 1:16–21).

For, "As He is, so are we in this world." (James 1:22–25; 1 John 4:17). Christ rose from the dead and we no longer "view Him as a mere Man." He is God, "King of kings and Lord of lords!" He died as a Man, "the Son of Man," but rose from the dead as the Son of the living God! (2 Corinthians 5:16–17).

God desires that we represent Him in the world so that all the good things that we need and long to possess can be made readily available for our enjoyment in accordance with the love He has commanded us to have for each other. And then, all other things will "fall into their proper place." (Matthew 5:9; 6:33).

"A new commandment I give to you, that you love one another; even as I have loved you, that you also love one another. By this all men will know that you are my disciples, if you have love for one another." (John 3:34–35).

Thus, as we understand "the Being of Christ," we ought to understand also how we ought to view, think of, and treat each other!

We are "born of God." Thus, we ought to pray for each other that Christ Jesus be continually "formed within us," so as to strengthen our Faith "in this world," and persevere in overcoming the "deceitful wiles of the devil;" "for we are not unaware of his evil designs." (2 Corinthians 2:9–11; 11:13–15).

Though we are "in this world," we are "not of this world." (1 Thessalonians 5:4–5; 1 John 3:14–18). What is physical is physical; but what is spiritual is spiritual! We are "of the first fruit of the risen from the dead," brothers and sisters in Christ Jesus, Abraham's Seed that was "planted in the ground" to rise again from the grave, for a bounteous harvest of faithful believers who would then imprint Christ's Truth upon the heart of every soul called by the purpose of God to be saved! (Romans 8:28–30; 10:8–13).

We are "born anew" in the Spirit, for overcoming, not only all the vicissitudes of our "Human Nature," but for also rendering void even "the false power" that Satan appears to have had obtained "in this world," not only through his deception of our Forbears, Adam and Eve, but also through exploiting such Human sinfulness as he had incited, for perpetrating the crucifixion of Christ. (1 Corinthians 2:6–10; 2 Corinthians 5:20–21). "For He who is in us is greater than he who is in the world." (1 John 4:4).

✶✶✶

HOW DO WE USE OUR FREE WILL?

WHAT DOES THAT MEAN: To be free; to have liberty; to have free will; to have freedom of volition? And we do have all these things — but, how do we utilize or "make usefulness" of them, when by ourselves, and when with other people in society?

"For it is for liberty that Christ has set us free; stand firm, therefore, and do not submit again to another yoke of bondage." (Galatians 5:1).

First, let's agree that there are "certain laws of Science," e.g., physics, chemistry, biology, and electrolytic nerve transmissions, that our body must observe, as we are exercising our Freedoms. Our hearts continue to beat regardless of the kinds of activities we are engaged in. Our blood still gets oxygenated for circulation to all our organs and body parts and members. Our lungs still extract Oxygen from earth Atmosphere to keep us breathing and alive. etc. . .

Therefore, The Holy Bible containing God's Word is "Spiritual-Scientific," for, as God's Spirit imparted "the Organizing Principle" to His Creation, Jesus Christ, His only begotten Son, is "the Way, the Truth and the Life." (John 14:6–7).

"The Organizing Principle" in the material-physical Universe, e.g., Law of gravitation; Law of Energy Transformation, etc. . ., is consistent with the indwelling of the Holy Spirit within us — endowing us with the "Organizing Principle" ruling "in the spirit realm" — to help us and empower us for living in accordance with God's righteous commandments of faith and works as we "do the Truth in love."

"Live as free men, yet without using your freedom as a pretext for evil. But live as servants of God." (1 Peter 2:16).

How we decide to enjoy our liberty through exercising our freedoms matters, not only for ourselves, but also for all members of society with whom we come into contact.

IT'S A CONTINUUM

The Devil had liberty and freedom while being an angel in Heaven. But he violated the trust that God had required of him. Thus, he was cast out of Heaven. He then took the form of a Serpent in the Garden of Eden in order to deceive our ancestors, Adam and Eve, into disobeying God's commandments.

Cain had murdered his brother Abel; that was, before the Law was given to Moses at Mount Sinai. Thus, Cain could "roam the earth" as a "vagabond," and no one could "bring him to justice." God would not allow it. But, after the Law came "on tablets of stone," God instituted corresponding punishment for deliberate wrongs committed upon the Earth. (Genesis 4:8–16; 20:1–26).

Every activity we perform, in everything we do, is in observance of "the Organizing Principle" that God embedded within the whole of His Creation. For examples: Our lungs must extract Oxygen from the atmosphere, and not Carbon Monoxide. We need water to stay alive, and not Sulfuric Acid. We need to eat foodstuff that will not poison us but will support and affirm our continual existence, until, hopefully, our natural death. We have to sleep every day, regularly, at specific times, in order to replenish our energies, rest, and renew our strength, as we pursue our activities of living, such as go to work, take care of our children, or go buy necessities at the store.

We are indeed "free to roam" on our Planet, not only within our own national borders but also as we travel around the world. "Freedom of movement" is one of the most crucial fundamental freedoms to which we do have a spiritual-scientific Right, and a natural Right.

"In the beginning God created the heavens and the earth. The earth was without form and void, and darkness was upon the face of the deep, and the Spirit of God was moving over the face of the waters." (Genesis 1:1–2).

"And the Spirit of God was moving over the face of the waters." Electrons continuously revolve around their atomic nucleus. The Earth continuously rotates daily upon its own 23.8 degree tilted axis within a 24-hour period, and continuously revolves around the Sun during 365 1/4 days a year. Rivers flow and seas roar with waves and tempest. Our seasonal cycles bring us weather accompanied by meteorological activities that produce rain, snow, windy storms, or gales of hail, depending upon geo-atmospheric conditions pertinent to each Season.

HOW DO WE USE OUR FREE WILL?

Our Minds are "also moving," as we are engaged in continuously thinking, apprehending, understanding and utilizing things around and about us that sustain and perpetuate our daily lives. (Romans 12:1-2; 1 Corinthians 2:14-16).

And, as experience has taught us, our society mirrors the natural necessity for laws that regulate our behavior, in the same manner that Nature has physical laws that regulate its environmental phenomena and ecological processes.

However, as we "roam free" in the Universe, we can love without fear, be bold without dissimulation, and be compassionate without selfish ends that would only "bloat our egos," even as we are being "charitable and generous." (Matthew 27:51; 2 Corinthians 12:19).

"The veil" has been removed from "our hearts of stone," as promised in the Old Testament by the Prophets; as the foreskin was removed "in circumcision." (Jeremiah 4:4; 9:25-26; 17:9-10; Ezekiel 36:26-27; Matthew 8:5-13; Luke 15:37-39; 2 Corinthians 3:12-18; 4:1-7; Philippians 3:2-3).

These were "the shadows of things to come," but the substance, the essential foundation, — "der Ding an sich," "the thing in itself," that is, "the Truth, the way, the life" — are all: Christ. (1 Corinthians 3:10-11; 2 Corinthians 3:3; 2 Corinthians 3:12-18; Galatians 4:19; Colossians 2:17-18).

The Universe as a whole is constituted of component parts, e.g., Galaxies, Star Systems, Solar systems, Planets, etc. . ., each, having its own specific role and function, within an organized order that proceeds in accordance with systemic laws, e.g., laws of physics, laws of chemistry, laws of electromagnetism, the law of gravitation; and laws regulating how our biological bodies respond to stimuli active within both our physical and social environments, which, in combination, include, not only the things we encounter in our natural ecology, but also those things which we ourselves have created, or "things of society," such as social institutions, organizations, relationships, and activities:

"We the People of the United States, in order to form a more perfect Union, establish justice, insure domestic tranquility, provide for the common defense, promote the general welfare, and secure the blessings of liberty to ourselves and our posterity, do ordain and establish this Constitution for the United States of America. (Constitution of the United States of America, 1787 AD).

As stated previously, the Constitution is ordained, written, and published for People, and not for "machines;" nor for "robots."

IT'S A CONTINUUM

"Things of Nature" and "things of society" at times meet or conjoin "to overtax" our abilities "to cope with" or "adapt to" our encompassing environments. Yet, the Holy Word of God's Truth in Christ Jesus states that we are indeed, not only "over-comers," but "more than conquerors," and not mere "adapters!" (Romans 8:37-39; 12:19-21; 1 John 5:3-5).

We are born of God, born of the Spirit in Jesus Christ. And Christ is "the Word made flesh." (John 1:14). Life is in the Spirit; the flesh is of no avail! (John 6:63; Galatians 6:13-18; Philippians 3:3). Thus, as God had said, as the Word had said with God, "Let there be light and there was light," the "Word made flesh" in us, "Christ, the Hope of Glory," can also say" "Be imitators of me as I am of Christ." (1 Corinthians 11:1). Christ, "the Word made flesh," can thus act in us, to transform us from within, unto His likeness not only for God's glory but also for our benefit and the well-being of our fellow Human Beings. Did not Christ heal and save the centurion's slave, by simply saying it? "I tell you, not even in Israel have I found such faith." And when those who had been sent to Jesus returned to the centurion's house, "they found the slave well." (Luke 7:1-10). Did not Christ raise Lazarus his friend from the dead by simply calling his name to come forth out of the tomb? (John 11:38-44).

But more than that, Christ lives within us, in our hearts. His voice is "not out there," but in us, as "the risen Word of God that WAS made flesh!" Christ is risen! He lives! Within us, to do according to His good pleasure in the will of our heavenly Father, Almighty God. (Romans 8:11; 10:1-4; 12:1-2; 14:7-9; Galatians 2:18-20).

When it snows in the winter, aren't there Human Beings, workers and laborers in our midst, "children of the living God," who utilize certain machines that plow the snow, so that pedestrians and vehicles can proceed, as "knowledge is increasing" and people are "going to and fro" in order to freely engage in their respective activities. (Daniel 12:4; Matthew 6:33; Luke 12:30-32).

Thus, both Nature and society operate "in accordance with laws" that pertain to each frame of reference, respectively. And in the same manner, that we continuously "move our bodies around" as we participate in our activities of daily living, our Minds continue "to move" as well, by "creating thoughts and forming ideas" related to fulfilling all our Human needs. Such thoughts and ideas pertaining to both "the abstract" and "the objective," such as analyzing a "relationship problem" that needs a solution; and

HOW DO WE USE OUR FREE WILL?

concrete physiological or biological prerogatives of living existence, such as deciding what to eat and when to go to sleep.

But "laws" are embedded within the Creation, so that all things may proceed according to God's plan; "laws" are willed by the Creator who brought the Creation into being by the power of His Spirit, by His spoken Word, in the presence of Christ, "the Word made flesh!"

Thus, God has established "the laws of Science!" "Science" as a system of "laws," e.g., Physics, whose "language" is mathematics, is deeply embedded within God's Creation, the whole Universe, from its very beginnings.

We are only "discovering" the mysterious Realities that God has already ordained and established into His whole Creation in Heaven and on the Earth for our benefit.

"Science," is merely an orderly way of organizing things in accordance with "laws" or "standards" necessary for applying "the Organizing Principle." Hence, why "Applied Sciences" must follow "theoretical Sciences" that have found "embodiment" in mathematical equations yielding useful technologies.

For example, an airplane utilizes principles enshrined in the Laws of Aerodynamics in order to "remain in the air" as it flies through Earth atmosphere in "scientific ways" that prevent it from falling to the ground! "Air pressure differentials" operate together "to give lift to the aircraft" as it glides through the air by the thrust of its engines, in response to pilot's commands affecting its fuselage, wings, ailerons, and flaps.

Our Minds, however, must belong to Christ whose Holy Spirit leads us unto all truths, as we are transformed by the renewing of our minds unto mature workmanship by the grace of God for loving Him and loving each other as Christ loves us. For "the whole law" is summed up in this: "Love your neighbor as yourself." (Mark 12:29-31; John 7:38; John 14:6; John 16:12-15; Romans 12:1-2; Galatians 5:13-15).

We are spirit-beings, primarily, and that's why God's spoken Word "works in us" to transform the World rather than to conform to its lusts, vices, and addictions.

God's Word spoken through the Apostle Paul in the Spirit of Christ tells us, that, the kinds of struggle, travails, tribulations, or troubles that we are faced with, "in this world," are "spiritual in nature."

Our weapons are not M16's or Uzis, but "spiritual weapons of righteousness" that bring down "strongholds" and bring every thought captive

IT'S A CONTINUUM

to obey Christ, even as we are "doing the Truth in love." (2 Corinthians 6:1-10; 10:3-6; Galatians 5:7-8; Ephesians 6:16-12).

Thus, though God "embedded the Sciences," into His Creation, e.g., Biology, Chemistry, and Physics, as well as the laws of gravity, and of electromagnetism, etc. . ., for our benefit and general welfare, the very essence of our Being as "spirit-creations," impels us onwards, as we ought to be, in "seeking-and-pursuing Christ-likeness;" first, in prayer, then in word, truth and deed, even as we are endeavoring to "invent new technologies" that alleviate, assuage, lighten, or allay the heavy burdens of our arduous labors, whether in "Agriculture," or in "Medicine."

Thus, the "set of fundamental organizing principles," that activate our "Science paradigm," together constituting our "scientific worldview," ought to flow from our understanding and knowledge of God's living Word of Truth in Christ's Holy Spirit — and not from "the elemental spirits of the Universe," e.g., the Planet, falsely called, "mother earth," from which we've been freed by Christ's resurrection from the dead! (Isaiah 1:18-20; 43:25-28; 45:18-23; 1 Corinthians 12:7; 12-13; 14:33; 2 Corinthians 13:5; 1 Thessalonians 5:19; 1 Timothy 6:20-21; 2 Timothy 1:6-7; 3:6-7; 1 John 4:1-3).

God gave us a deep understanding of His love for us that surpasses all knowledge, — "this indescribable blessing," "this unspeakable endowment," "this inexpressible gift," — through empowerment of our hearts by His Spirit in Christ Jesus, because, firstly, we were created "in His own image and likeness" which Christ "embodied" in-the-flesh when He lived amongst us as a "Human," as a "Man," as "the Son of Man," and whose Holy Spirit lives within us because of His resurrection from the dead and His ascension unto Heaven!

As Christ loves us, the Father is also loving us, in such unfathomable ways that inspire us with awe and wonderment, so that we can also learn to love each other as He loves us. With such assurances, we can continue to resist that "defeated foe," the Devil whose wicked works of evil were destroyed by Christ's resurrection from the dead, after which, He then ascended unto Heaven, to sit at the right hand of power of God. (Romans 8:37-39; 16:19-20; 2 Corinthians 9:13-15; 2 Timothy 2:8-13; Colossians 1:13-20; Philippians 4:4-7; James 4:7-8; 2 Peter 5:6-10).

Love is not a mere "feeling" that our physiological organism emotes. Love is an action, and not a mere "transient emotion."

HOW DO WE USE OUR FREE WILL?

Genuine love, love without dissimulation, is, true love that acts in accordance with "Christ-likeness," overflowing from our inner-being, for an outpouring of blessedness in good works and honest deeds towards others, our fellow Human Beings, and towards ourselves, sum of which, transcending and over-coming our irrational fleshly passions that tend towards self-deprecation and self-destruction, which, not only harm us, but also injure our neighbors, other Human Beings in society. (Romans 12:9; 1 Corinthians 15:58; Colossians 3:23–25;).

Our bodies are physical but our Minds are abstract. Our spirit lives as our soul "walks and acts in righteousness." But "we walk by faith, not by sight." (2 Corinthians 5:7).

The Universe and the Earth are physical, but within their operations are embedded comprehensible applicable "laws" that we understand in an abstract way, that is yet, consistent and confluent, with objectively observed ecological processes, thermodynamics, energy transformation, and other natural phenomena, which, at different times in our lives, might be "occupying our attention," as "embodied" in mathematical equations, such as, $f = ma$; $E = mc^2$; $F = G\, m_1 m_2/r^2$.

In short, this mysterious fact of wondrous Reality, — that our abstractions might correspond to observed natural phenomena — is a "dualism" from which we cannot escape; nor can we avoid. In Human living, on the Earth and the Universe, we face, acknowledge, reckon or "deal with," abstract invisible "laws" that objectively describe, regulate, and govern, visible objective activities in which both Nature, and we, engage.

Both the Christian and the "Existentialist" must accept abstract principles of morality that govern how we relate to each other and how we transact with our environment; though such "Existentialists" might deny that their origin is from God. We subscribe to "laws of civility," as much as we establish "laws of sanitation." Treating each other with Human dignity and decency, is as important as disposing of waste generated during our daily biological, social, and industrial activities.

Our relationships with God and with one another, ought to, above all, take precedence, over all other forms of activities. For, what is flesh is flesh; what is spirit, is spirit! Spirit is primary as flesh is secondary: Flesh "responds to initiatives" or "directives" of the spirit!

In every form of experience having to do with social activities, whether at universities or at the road construction site, we are associating with Human Beings like ourselves, albeit mortal, but still, spirit-beings predisposed

IT'S A CONTINUUM

to be "in communion with" our heavenly Father, the same who sent Christ to empower us for His glory, exhorting us to live as created: as "born anew Christians," as "new creations" who are "born of the Spirit," "born of God." (Isaiah 42;6–9; 43:18; 48;6; 62:2; 66:22; John 1:12–13; 3:3; John 3:16; John 17:3; Romans 6:1–4; 12:1–2).

So, you see: We can't help being a "spiritual-moral people" with a "spiritual-scientific outlook," even when we find ourselves to be attempting to deny it.

We are able to go through transformations in mind, soul, spirit, and heart, so that as we change our ways, we are renewing ourselves in life-affirming commitments that glorify God and preserve our "way of living:" Not only our spiritual life, but also our biological existence. And, That, being, not "godless secular humanism;" but the miraculous heavenly gift of a "Christ-centered Humanism." (John 1:14; 2:23–25; 1 Corinthians 7:31; 2 Corinthians 5:16–21).

As "the Speed of Light," has a "limit: It is 186,000 miles per second! So too, we, also must face "limits and boundaries" in our spiritual activities, relations with our physical-ecological environment, and our moral relationships to one another.

As we "walk with God" and "transact with" each other, we must acknowledge that we are only "passing through," this, our physical natural environment, which we call "The Universe." Living in newness of life means that: True Love comes to life through action, and is not a mere transient feeling or temporary emotion! (Romans 6:1–4; 9–11).

Hence, why we are entreated "to DO the truth in love," through this commandment by Christ: That, in His Holy Spirit, we love each other as He and God, His father, our father, also love us.

"That kind of world," yes, we can build, even as we're laboring for God's kingdom, as "Forgiven Builders," but in faithful and righteous service to our Savior, and also, in service to each other. No other fulfillment or achievement is greater than giving glory to God through our earthly service to Him and to one another! (John 13:34–35; Galatians 2:18–20.)

Certain categories of things that exist are inescapably replete with "limits and boundaries," e.g., our capabilities to think and reason are flawed and therefore prone to error. There are also commonly experienced restrictions imposed upon our behavior and activities, such as "by inclement weather."

Thus, Liberty does not mean "random chaos." Nor does freedom mean "godless anarchy!" Hence, why we say, "No one is above the law!"

"Laws of Physics" are believed to be operating in ways that govern "how the Universe works," even as Christ's commandments must govern our "way of life" on the Earth.

Therefore, our earthly experiences, in this well-organized Creation, within which God continues to bless and prosper us, are always "Spiritual-Scientific."

God spoke, and the Universe is! In the same manner, the United States of America, was born according to these transcendent spiritual and moral principles effectuated through "spiritual-scientific reasoning."

"When in the course of human Events, it become necessary for one people to dissolve the political bands which had hitherto connected them with another, and to assume among the powers of the Earth, the separate and equal Station to which the laws of Nature and of Nature's God entitle them, a decent Respect to the Opinions of Mankind requires that they should declare the Causes which impel them to the Separation.

"We hold these Truths to be self-evident, That all men are created equal, That they are endowed by their Creator with certain inalienable Rights, That among these are Life, Liberty, and the pursuit of Happiness — That to secure these Rights, Governments are instituted among Men, deriving their just powers from the consent of the governed, " (Declaration of Independence of the United States of America, July 4th, 1776).

That's our God-endowed "Socio-political paradigm!" It is God-centered! From this framework of God-anchored organizing principles patterned after biblical inspiration must our constitutional enactments flow in order to agree with the ends of Justice, Peace, and Equality. (Deuteronomy 10:12–20; Psalms 8:4–6; Micah 6:8; Acts 10:34–38; Romans 2:6–11; Galatians 2:1–11).

In the same vein, it is only through "the Organizing Principle" that the Law of Transformation of Energy can proceed, as both Conservation and Entropy. It is through the "Organizing Principle" embedded within the Declaration of Independence that, not only the Constitution can remain "the Supreme law of the Land," but also, that our system of free government can overcome all obstacles that may come our way. (Deuteronomy 6:4–9; 19:15; Colossians 3:23–25; 2 Timothy 3:14–17; Titus 3:3–8).

Application of a "law," must be consistent with its letter, spirit, and context. For example, The Laws of Thermodynamics proceed in operations

IT'S A CONTINUUM

that must apply within "a range of values" that are consistent with their "limits and boundaries," so as to accomplish their respective purposes.

This "range of values" has "effectiveness," that is, to the extent that they are self-sufficient in fulfilling the ends-in-view of operational processes as purposed, e.g., the PH of Water is 7; the rate of gravitational acceleration on the Earth proceeds at 9.88 meters per second squared; the Speed of Light is 186,000 miles per second; One Earth rotation takes 24 hours; One Earth revolution around the Sun takes 1 year, etc. . .

Thus, "This self-sufficient range of effective values" for fulfilling paradigmatic purposes within a specific frame-of-reference, consists of steps or stages as necessitated by pertinent processes that are not only limited in number, but are also bounded by duration.

Each parameter or variable has a "quantitative rate of change," as measured in accordance with its occurrence within a certain Time-frame, e.g., Planet Earth rotates upon its own 23.8-degree tilted axis during a period of 24 hours or one day, sum of which, allowing one planetary hemisphere to be "bathed in Sunlight," as the other hemisphere is "enveloped in darkness," — absence of Star-light — so that ecological processes can fulfill their purposes, according to their respectively prescribed limits and boundaries.

Time, or "processing duration," measures "rates of change" in system parameters or variables. "Processing time," during which variables (e.g., gallons or liters of fuel) are operating within their prescribed "ranges of values," (e.g., miles or kilometers per hour) is imposed upon "thermodynamic events," e.g., amount of fuel consumption by an engine running during an hour of vehicular travel, that must have a beginning, a period of processing, and an end, as they are producing "a final output," e.g., covering a specific distance in kilometers or miles.

One complete Earth rotation upon its own tilted axis, in conjunction with the Moon remaining in synchronized rotation, takes 24 hours or one day; One complete Earth revolution around the Sun takes approximately 365 1/4 days or one year, sum of which, combined with solar radiation, are accountable for Earth "ecological life-support systems."

We utilize "clocked Time," only to measure "rates of change" occurring in "system variables," in accordance with God's operational design for our organized Universe.

"Rates of change" apply to every thermodynamic parameter or variable participating in controlling every System organized to operate in accordance with "intrinsic laws," "instructions," or "information," as embedded, whether within ecological Nature on the Earth, or within organic processes pertinent to our Organisms or biological bodies; or, as well as, within our Minds and in the Universe-at-large, e.g., Our self-iterative System of earthly Seasonal Cycles; our cardiovascular system; our endocrine system; our system of free government; our free enterprise economic system; our Solar System.

"Clocked-time" or "operational duration," is embedded within the span of eternal Time, e.g., God is eternal, that is, God has no beginning and no end (Eternity); but a Human Being might be born in 1921 and might eventually die in 1992, for a life-span of Seventy-One years (Temporality).

But, even as we utilize "clocked time" to measure "rates of change" in system variables, we learn that, God has "put Eternity," irrefutably, as well, "in our hearts!" (Ecclesiastes 1:9; Ecclesiastes 3:10–11; John 17:3; Romans 8:19–24; 1 John 2:22–25.) Though living only temporarily on the Earth, we possess discernment of a "certain sense of permanence" attached to the Universe, which we must "leave behind," even as we "had found it" or "discovered it," at the time of our birth.

"Transient time" or "clocked time" is embedded within the Continuum of Eternity! We live temporarily, i.e., we have a beginning from conception and birth, a process of development, growth and maturity into a "life-span," that then terminates or ends in death — while God, our Creator Himself, is eternal — God has always existed; He has no beginning and no end!

But for us mortals, Christ is "the beginning and the end," "the first and the last," "the Alpha and the Omega" who "knows the end, from the beginning." Christ was also present at the time God created the whole Universe. (Genesis 1:26–28; Exodus 3:13–14; Isaiah 46:10; Revelation 1:8; 22:12–16).

We can only eat "so much;" and can sleep only "so long." We can only labor for certain "amounts of time," as permitted by our age and allowed by our health status, after which, rest, relaxation, and recreation are necessitated.

A tank of gasoline will eventually become empty as motorized operations of a vehicle utilize the fuel for its combustive processes.

Yes, we are indeed free "spirit-beings." But we must follow certain "natural laws" that sustain and affirm our living existence, as well as "socio-political economic laws" that govern our earthly existence, as citizens of a nation.

In order to do all these things "the right way," that is, without harm or injury to self or others, we must also follow moral commandments embedded within spiritual principles of righteous living, as ordained by God and as established by our Lord and Savior Jesus Christ (Jus, juris), in accordance with which we attempt to enact laws or "pass legislation," so that our form of civilized way of life might continually persist on the Earth, from generation to generation (Lex, legis), e.g., Thou shalt not steal; Thou shalt not commit murder, etc...

Is there "a relationship," or correspondence, between "physical laws" embedded in Nature and "socio-political laws" such as those governing our economic system of free enterprise, or system of free government, for example? Certainly!

Every System process that pertains to every event or thing that exists in the Universe, must operate within a certain specific "range of values," as prescribed by limits and as encompassed by boundaries!

Those divinely inspired principles and commandments present certain "limits and boundaries," — consistent with "the laws of physical-material Nature" governing our ecological and cosmic environments, — that we must observe, even as we "Do the Truth in love;" respective to how we fulfill our innate needs of daily living, as well as to the periods of time during which we can engage in certain specific physical and social activities, e.g., We are commanded to glorify our Creator all the days of our lives; and thus, we do pause from our labors, as we observe a special day of Christian worship every week, on Sunday! For, even "the Lord rested on the Seventh day!" (Genesis 2:1–3; 1 Corinthians 8:5–6; 13:8–13; 15:32–34; 2 Corinthians 5:10; 5:14–15; 2 Timothy 3:16; Titus 2:7–8; Titus 2:11–14.)

Operating according to "abstract laws" demand prescribed limits and boundaries that allow every System to engage within a specific range of activities, e.g., the Human Organism, our body, must follow certain laws of nutrition in order to remain relatively healthy.

"Laws" that maintain a System in fulfillment of its purposefully designed Objectives, must be so consistent as to allow each component, each part, each member, or its constituent parameter, to perform its specific function in accordance with its own embedded characteristics, as required by the System as a whole. "For God is not the author of confusion, but of peace as in all the churches of the saints." (1 Corinthians 14:33). Thus, consistency, infallibility, and inerrancy in "embodying spiritual-scientific Truth," within the whole System, must be preserved, e.g., The heart has its own function for maintaining our cardio-vascular blood-circulation System, just as the lungs have their own function in providing our bodies

HOW DO WE USE OUR FREE WILL?

with a "blood-Oxygenation System," respectively, as they BOTH subscribe to the biological laws of life that govern, as a Whole, all our physiological processes.

Likewise, in Human society, all things have "a certain connectedness" that sustain the vitality of the whole constitutional "system of laws," consistent with our form of free government, via "social structures" within which are embedded: customs, mores, traditions, usage, instructions, or values, that are "consensually enacted," in order to regulate "the forms of civilized behavior" we can engage in.

Certain "laws" — , i.e., instructions, principles, rules, or doctrines (lex, legis, or "enacted legislation") given as necessary to each part for just and peaceful acquisition of property, — prescribed in order to "do something right" so as to achieve a specific purpose, as consistent with maintaining stability, continuum, and durability of the System as a Whole, — (Jus, juris or "the whole body of law" or constitutional Jurisprudence), e.g., "Thou shalt not commit murder;" "Thou shalt not steal," — that we consent to or agree upon, will govern how we fulfill our innate needs for security, safety, freedom, peace, justice, family, and equality, for examples, by ensuring that all members of our society have complete lawful access to all legal ways-and-means, avenues and resources, for acquiring "Life-enhancing property," such as Food, Water, Clothing, Shelter, Medical Care, and Education — while, at the same time, making provisions for enabling our capacities "to engage in other activities" that allow us "to be moving," — such as some forms of "recreational activities," or of "regular exercise" combined with "nutritional prerogatives," — sum of which, allowing us to regulate how we maintain the vibrancy of our health, lest our arteries be clogged, thus predisposing our Organism to "Metabolic Syndrome," from which may arise our contracting "Type-2 Diabetes;" suffering from "a stroke," or failing from a "heart attack."

Evidently, then, Human Life in the Universe and on the Earth, is "Thermodynamic." That means: Our "way of life" is "Spiritual-Scientific!"

All physiological processes and social activities must submit to the "Input-Process-Output Mechanism" activating our mental health, spiritual maturity, educational development, professional preparation, as well as, our in-toto biological functioning and organic operations.

Thus, our subscribing to this "thermodynamic Mechanism," that is, "Input-Process-Output," is inevitable and unavoidable. Not only must our bodies be fed in the "natural way," but our hearts and our minds must also

IT'S A CONTINUUM

obtain "spiritual nourishment." For, "processing for specific Outputs" or results, is occurring, respectively, in all these spheres of Human activities! In the first one, for "healthy digestion" that sustains our innate needs for metabolic energies; and in the second, "civilized behavior" that sustains our innate needs for life, liberty, love, peace, justice, security, safety, freedom, equality, and prosperity.

It also means that all variables and parameters that factor into keeping us alive will offer "rates of change" defining "a pattern of cycling operations," having: A beginning; a period or duration of processing; and a purpose and an end, e.g., we eat to get hungry again; we sleep in order to work, after which, we get tired, thus, needing sleep again.

But, those "stochastic thermodynamic cycling patterns of Input processing" are embedded within a "consistent Stream or wellspring" that propagates during an all life-long Continuum; hence, our organism having a "life-span," in the same manner that the radiation Energy Spectrum might be in the Forms of either a particle or a wave, respectively; or that "temporary time," "clocked time," or "periodic cycles" are embedded within the framework of Time Eternal, or Eternity. A line is a Continuum formed by "succession of particular-singular dots!"

We nourish our Bodies and our Minds for healthy functioning, in order to obtain proper levels of mental and physiological Energy that allow us "to do work" or "perform activities" pertaining to and consistent with, "living well," on Planet Earth, i.e., "having nothing," i.e., we leave it all behind when we eventually die, that is, "No U-Haul behind a Hearse;" but yet, "not lacking anything," i.e., We live peaceably and prosperously, with an all-encompassing envelope or frame of loving and compassionate relationships, in accordance with "just powers from the consent of the governed."

"Having nothing" and yet "not lacking anything!" Another mysterious but most wondrous paradox! Is it? Still, is it not what Holy Bible Scriptures are all about?

But living on Planet Earth is rife with "limits and boundaries," affecting the "ranges of operations" or "patterns of activities," we can engage in, framing how we perform them, and as consistent with their respective durations.

These analytical observations reflect the complexity of maintaining stability and durability for Continuum Human Civilization, sums of which, have led to certain philosophical discourses addressing "this perplexing

HOW DO WE USE OUR FREE WILL?

conundrum" or framing "this vexing paradox," in terms of: "Freedom and Necessity."

Do we still have freedoms to enjoy within these necessary limits and boundaries? Of course, we do. And rightly so!

The very establishment of those "necessary limits and boundaries" for our conduct and behavior, is an indication of exercising our Liberty in utilizing the Organizing Principle that inheres in the Universe, to our benefit and advantage, and to the disparagement of no one.

In spite of all the "limits and boundaries" imposed upon Nature that frame our Biology and our Social Systems, we still possess the God-given liberty to enjoy many freedoms that enhance our physiological health, spiritual well-being, and mental welfare, for a prosperous, peaceful, just and principled "way of life." "Life more abundant," as we patiently await "Life eternal!"

Thus, to oppose "Freedom and Necessity" in a "false tug of war" is not too constructive, "not too realistic," and not too beneficial, given that "there is no escaping" the necessary intermingling and entangling co-dependence of the two with each other. Superposing them as "opposites" rather than "complements," renders summation of our lives more difficult, whereas, "the whole law and the prophets are summed up in this: You shall love your neighbor as yourself." (Galatians 5:1–26).

For example, our current "state of Space-flight technology" cannot take us to other Planets, or has not yet, made it possible for us to get out of our own Planet Earth, let alone, out of our own Solar System.

Thus, in spite of the vast expansiveness of the Universe as a Whole, within which we can "roam free" on the Earth and beyond, we still have "spatial limitations." Our Atmosphere, even at "low earth orbits," appears to present "a Form of physical boundary" or "spatial limit," to both our willingness to explore "where no Human has gone before," and our "current level" or "current progress" in sophisticated or advanced technologies.

The Planet has a spheroid volume that contains a land surface, an atmosphere, and oceans. Appropriate technologies of atmospheric flight include rotary blades, such as for the helicopter; winged propeller-thrust aircraft; winged aircraft with "jet engines" or "turbines;" and rockets ignited or fueled by compressed or enclosed explosive gases or liquids, such as Hydrogen or Oxygen, out of which, egress exhaust gases with vanes, allowing for controlling the direction and path of the rockets.

IT'S A CONTINUUM

Thus, the plane (propeller or jet powered), the helicopter, and the rocket-ship constitute atmospheric flight technologies prevalent in our times.

However, only the rocket-ship type of propulsion System can function in "non-atmospheric" or in "void-Space" or "non-Oxygenated Space."

But due to fuel and payload limitations, the rocket-ship, thus far, has not afforded us to "space-travel" so as to be capable of reaching other Planets or leaving our Solar System. We can send space-probes working as "telescoping robots" in cosmic Space, that, in due time, with electronic telemetry, can transmit "photographed information" or "radio-logically obtained observations" back to Earth.

Building a rocket-ship with enough payload and fuel capacity, would be so big, that it would result in a "huge flying fuel tank" that still would not allow astronauts to travel to another Planet, such as Mars, and to then return to Earth; and given the span of astronomical distances that must be covered, this type of huge rocket-ship flying-fuel- tank technology has proven to be "unpractical."

In short, we need to invent a new Form of spacecraft propulsion system that efficiently resolves rocket-ship size, payload platform, and fuel capacity problems.

Nuclear-powered technologies are being explored. However, given the critical dangers of an accidental explosion that could incinerate large areas of the country, this option has not been pursued to any practical applications or scientific uses.

Those "spatial limitations" might even lure and enthrall some of us to think of the Earth as "the biggest prison" for Human Beings in our Solar System: Simply because we can't go to other Planets, yet; simply because "we can't get out of it," yet.

Is the Earth truly the biggest open prison-system for Humans? Not necessarily! Technologies considering!

There are also limits to "Human endurance" or to the "amount of stress" that we can take, excessive levels of which, can overwhelm our body's capacities to "cope with" or "adapt to" environmental changes or natural phenomena. For example, Given that we are "naked from birth" or that we have "no covering" such as birds that have feathers and turtles that have carapaces, we must wear warm clothing during the winter months of the year, e.g., we call some of our clothing sweaters and coats.

HOW DO WE USE OUR FREE WILL?

In the same vein, in Nature, certain foodstuff might be deadly if eaten, such as "poison mushrooms," in the same manner that, in society, Carbon Monoxide emitted from inefficient motorized vehicular engines might climax into injurious illnesses or even death, such as in experiencing pulmonary dysfunctions, or contracting cancer.

But apart from these, "Human Relationships," being the most complex of all relations in this "intelligent-Life" or "Human-centered Universe," present the greatest opportunities for stressful conditions that can overtax our capacities to thrive and prosper on the Earth, "as our soul prospers!" (3 John 1–15). Hence, our innate need for Jesus Christ as the "spiritual Physician," or "the author and finisher of our faith!" (Hebrews 12:1–11).

"Input-Process-Output," is, "the thermodynamic mechanism" operating within the framework of every System, respectively, with limits and boundaries that restrict activities in each frame of reference, within only "a range of operations" or "a range of values," consistent with its design, structure, organizational arrangement, end-in-view, or processes aimed at "fulfillment of a certain specific purpose," e.g., It is recommended that we sleep at least 8 hours a day in order to get "properly refreshed" or "healthily rejuvenated" in both mental and physiological Energies, so as to be ready and prepared, for taking care of "next day's business."

And, yet, Machines or Robots can only do so much! They, also, need periodic repairs or replacements, if not continuous maintenance! And given the vastness and complexity of our universal environment, Human physiological capacities have limited development and bounded applications. "Superman" and "Superwoman" are "placebo fictions" that entertain our mutual needs for palliative commiseration and cathartic ego-boosting! However, "the Spirit is not chained;" "the Word of God is not fettered;" "the Word of God is not bound!" (John 3:31–36; 16:12–15; Ephesians 5:11–20; 2 Timothy 2:8–19).

In addition, more pressing an imperative, is that, social institutions or political organizations wherein is embedded the exercise of constitutionally granted powers, such as our form of free government, must also have certain "limits and boundaries" that regulate "the portent of the exercise of such granted powers," as well as set the limits to which such powers can be exercised, so as to safeguard the constitutionally-centered, administrative functioning and operational activities of our consensually established, freely ordained, and peaceably organized public institutions, structures, systems, and organizations, e.g., through such "auxiliary precautions" as

IT'S A CONTINUUM

division of powers, separation of powers, checks-and-balances, voting, elections, public oversight, open meetings and hearings, periodic reports from each governmental agency, etc...

Our form of free government operates with certain "mechanisms of self-control" that, when applied properly, must prevent concentration of all powers into the same hands, which would then result in a "dictatorship" with despotic uses of unjust powers; and, at the same time, such "regulatory mechanisms of self-restraint," must also thwart the emergence of lawlessness, anarchy, or "mob rule." Thus, our system of free government is ordained and established to not only avert "despotic rule" but to also prevent "mob rule!"

Hence, the principle that — In order to secure our inalienable, constitutional, God-endowed Rights, our form of free government has been instituted such that, as a system of free government, it can only obtain, just powers from our consent, or "just powers from the consent of the governed."

In addition to reliance upon We the People as its foundation for exercising granted powers, our government is constitutionally comprised of three branches — the Legislative, the Executive, and the Judicial — that must operate administratively within certain provisions prescribing self-control and self-restraint, such as above-listed, "checks-and-balances," "division of powers," "due process of law," and "separation of powers," thus, imposing limits and boundaries that constrain the unjust exercise of constitutionally granted powers so that WE THE PEOPLE continue to guard and secure, protect, preserve, and defend, not only our "substantive rights," but also our "due-process rights."

As one of our Founders, James Madison, puts it:

"Justice is the end of government. It is the end of civil society. It ever has been and ever will be pursued until it be obtained, or until liberty be lost in the pursuit." (James Madison, Publius/Federalist Papers No. 51).

But, the God-endowed Liberty to enjoy numerous Freedoms also has certain "ranges of lawful exercise." We are still predestined to possess the God-given Liberty to freely enjoy a lot of various and diverse activities, with "wide latitude and breadth," even within the self-imposed "limits and boundaries" that control "the ranges of freedoms" we can engage in, e.g., we do have an inalienable right to lawfully, peaceably, and justly obtain or acquire material possessions and property, but without lawlessly stealing, unjustly destroying, or violently killing for them, e.g., "bank robbers" or "arsonists" are "put in jail" in accordance with "due process of law."

As we have "physical limits" and "spatial limits," we also experience "legal boundaries" within which we must freely exercise our constitutional Bill-of-Rights freedoms, e.g., We enjoy "freedom of movement," but when driving a vehicle, we must observe "Rules of the Road" that proscribe driving through "a red light." For, "a red light" signifies: Stop! until the light is "green again;" meaning, after which, that we can continue driving towards our intended or purposed destination.

Such are the ways in which "civilized living" is framed in accordance with "just powers from the consent of the governed," sums of which, embodied in "laws, regulations, statutes, policies, and rules" to which we freely agree and willingly consent to observe, follow, and abide by.

For example, only birds can fly through the atmosphere! But we can still build aircrafts to "fly through the atmosphere," even though we are not birds!

We cannot run or gallop as fast as a horse, but we create machines such as automobiles that can run faster than a horse on the surface of the Earth.

The machines we create are only "extensions" of a respective Human capacity whose "limits and boundaries" we are attempting to overcome, e.g., we are capable of "walking and running," and thus, by first using horses for transportation; and then, as technological developments are advanced or improved, we utilize trains, planes or automobiles that are manufactured "to extend the scope" of such innate biological physiological capabilities.

We can perform arithmetic operations in our Minds. Thus, we even invented "calculators" to help us immediately compute abstract mathematical problems and solve difficult equations that would take our Minds, otherwise, longer durations for operationally processing the required steps towards obtaining accurate solutions and forthright results.

Machines are "convenient," in that they operate much faster, and sometimes, more accurately. But, these machines can also "break down." Their creators, Humans, are flawed; so are their machines! Entropy, often, rules the day!

Regarding this vexatious paradox, which we call, "Human Nature" which is partly accountable for our "Human Condition," James Madison, American Founder, in the same Publius/Federalist Papers, Article, No. 51, states:

IT'S A CONTINUUM

"But what is government itself but the greatest of all reflections on human nature. If men were angels, no government would be necessary. If angels were to govern men, neither external nor internal controls on government would be necessary. In framing a government which is to be administered by men over men, the great difficulty lies in this: you must first enable the government to control the governed; and in the next place oblige it to control itself."

Thus, "from the diaper to the coffin," though we must face "limits and boundaries" that confine our activities as framed within "a range of operations" during which they can be freely enjoyed and effectually exercised, we still possess the broadest spectrum of God-given liberty to act deliberately, openly, freely, and willingly, within "the wide expanse of the Planet," or even within the vast immense purview or breadth of the extant Universe, as befitting each respective "range of freedom" or "degree of freedom," e.g., We have an orbiting Space-station that requires extreme precautions for temporarily habiting therein such that our astronauts are protected against extreme doses of solar radiation as well as long periods of inactivity, which, otherwise, would be accountable for loss of bone density, and of muscle tone, as well as, hypercalcuria (or the loss of minerals such as Calcium, sums of which, that cumulatively calcify within the Human body such that kidney functions might be impaired).

Thus, consistent with the good purposes for which we desire to act, we freely, prudently, cautiously, lawfully, justly, safely, willingly, and peaceably proceed to perform various or diverse activities, sums of which, pertaining to beneficent fulfillment of our real needs or constructive desires, respectively.

From learning how to say "dada" and "mama," to learning to resolve complex mathematical equations; from being able to only run a few miles to landing on the Moon, these cycles of activities, or self-iterative patterns of operations, must all observe "certain limits and boundaries," respective to their own principled category, or System of organized order.

James Madison, American Founder, continues, regarding why government must be "obliged to control itself:"

"A dependence on the people is, no doubt, the primary control on the government; but experience has taught mankind the necessity of auxiliary precautions." (Publius/ Federalist Papers, No. 51).

So, dear friends, consistent with these "auxiliary precautions," our system of free government, — framed as "the administration of Humans over

Humans," — is also accompanied by an inalienable Bill of Rights, applicable to us all, as embedded within the very textual content of our Constitution, in word, letter, deed and spirit; sums of which, we firmly hold, as our much-cherished, God-endowed, "wellspring of living spiritual-moral principles" instructing us and informing our actions, for self-government, self-control, temperance, self-restraint, and self-regulation.

These "auxiliary precautions" that are enshrined for observance in our daily lives, are necessary for effectual, socio-economic operations and political administration, as well as, for safeguarding, protecting, defending, and preserving, the very entrails of the Constitution of the United States of America and our inalienable Bill of Rights contained-and-packaged therein, sums of which, being "the supreme law of the land!"

Regrettably, despite "the laws" that govern, regulate, or control our natural and social activities within operations and processes having "ranges of freedoms" because of our essentially flawed "Human nature;" and in spite of the fact that such freely self-imposed restrictions must need be due to Entropy in physical-natural processes: Still, we enjoy the broadest array or the widest spectrum of our God-given Liberty, within those very self-regulating principles, for as long as we live; even as we are predisposed to err, and predestined for biological death!

That's the perennial paradox of "Freedom and Necessity" with which we must live, as well as, with which we must prosper, "as our soul prospers," for enjoying "all the good things that are ours in Christ Jesus" who "reconciles" us to our Heavenly Father on whom we can lay our heavy burdens and stressful troubles. (Matthew 11:27–29; Philippians 1:6–11; 1 Thessalonians 5:23–24; Philemon 6; 3 John 1–3).

How do we "learn to behave in a civilized manner?" Well, forgive us for reiterating these veracities emblematic of our "Human Condition:" It begins with the diapers, continues within those freely self-imposed self-regulations during the time we're developing, growing-up, maturing and aging, and ends with the honorary burial in a coffin at the cemetery of our choice!

Consequently, what we teach, how we learn, what we learn, and how we act, are all related to the constructive ways in which we respond to the "limits and boundaries" that regulate our behavior, within "the ranges of freedoms" that we enjoy, even as we endeavor to self-impose, self-govern, self-regulate, or self-control; but, in spite of which, at times, it still might regrettably result, in not preventing some of us from "becoming less civilized"

IT'S A CONTINUUM

than others, e.g., Our society is also full of "criminals" jailed in accordance with due process of law who are caught willfully "violating these limits and boundaries" as enshrined in "the rule of law."

In the same vein, as the Holy Scriptures affirm: Wars of violence for hostile conquests appear to predominate in the annals of Human History on this Planet we call "Earth!" — That is, until we learn to cultivate "the peace of Christ ruling in our hearts." (John 14:27; Romans 16:18–20; Colossians 3:1–25; Philippians 2:12–17; 4:4–13).

Otherwise, as historically affirmed in the Holy Bible:

(From the times of the Prophets, given that John the Baptist was a Prophet, the last Prophet to come while "the children of Israel" were still under the Old Covenant) "From the days of John the Baptist until now the kingdom of heaven suffers violence, and the violent take it by force. For all the Prophets and the law prophesied until John." (Matthew 11:12–13).

Violence towards each other for theft of material possessions or physical property; or murdering and killing each other by war for "conquests of spoils," begins in the Human heart where thoughts of cruel hatred and prejudicial plans of hostility burgeon as based upon certain aspects of the ways in which we are affected by our Sinfulness and by Entropy e.g., by "the love of money" which the Word of God says is "the root of all sorts of evil;" by serving "the mammon of unrighteousness" rather than serving God; through covetousness and greed, ill will, demonic deception, underhanded lies, or devious schemes of violence to acquire, steal, or confiscate, "for possessing and owning what does not belong to us." (Matthew 6:22–24; 1 Timothy 6:9-10; 2 Timothy 3;1–9; James 4:1–10).

Disheartening and disconcerting as it is, "the murderous spirit of Cain" appears to still have "some sort of grip" upon the hearts of some people amongst us whose minds would, indeed, need to be "transformed" unto the righteousness of God through the knowledge of the inexpressible riches of the glory of Christ Jesus! (2 Corinthians 9:6–15).

For even "after crimes upon crimes," such "Cain-spirited people" do eventually die, to leave behind and permanently lose, all that they've acquired in "frenzied feats of conquests" while spreading suffering, pain, and misery in their wake, as they've persisted in "scrounging-and-scratching-and-scavenging" for such transient, temporary "loot and booty," while destructively wasting their Souls during the span of their most precious gift and blessing from God, our loving Creator: Their whole life-time! e.g., Caesar, Alexander, Hitler, Stalin, and many others.

HOW DO WE USE OUR FREE WILL?

And for what? Does violent conquest of "spoils, loot, and booty" ever bring about or result in also "stealing the Tree of Life," sealed in the resurrection power of our Savior and Lord Jesus Christ? No! Not ever!

Do such "crimes upon crimes" ultimately bestow BIOLOGICAL IN-THE-FLESH IMMORTALITY upon those lawless perpetrators? No, not ever!

But their odious crimes continue to painfully hurt the very people who have to "mop up the mess" they've created, as engraved in their memory, seared in their moral conscience, and imprinted in their minds, to engender the most hideous of all forms of Stress: P.T.I.S, or "Post-Traumatic Injury Syndrome," otherwise called "Post-Traumatic Stress Disorder" or P.T.S.D.

But the Word of God entreats us to first seek the kingdom of God and His righteousness so that we can then freely obtain those things that fulfill our real needs in a peaceful, just, and lawful manner. (Matthew 6:33; James 3:16–18).

Consequently, we can learn how to utilize or govern the ways in which our emotions take control of our thoughts and actions, which is referred to as "emotional intelligence."

Other Human Beings called "philosophers" might frame this innate capacity for "emotional intelligence," in terms of our mere "living through experiences" we meet "from the diaper to the coffin:" As "we adapt" to the numerous conditions intrinsic to our various environments.

Others, such as Socio-biologists, even contend that we have to learn self-discipline, self-abnegation, selflessness, or self-control via "operant conditioning," or through a "system of rewards and punishments" whereby each form of behavior is either positively reinforced or negatively discouraged through "the pain and pleasure principle." Of course, this "paradigm of motivation," otherwise referred to as "Pavlovian conditioning," was instituted from observations accrued in torturing laboratory rats with electric shock to force them to drink water, even when they're not thirsty, which professors teach students at universities, who happen, as well, to be "the victims doing the torturing," while enrolled in "Psychology 101."

However, God has always been present in Human History, even when perceived as "absent" by evil doers who appear to prevail for a time. (Leviticus 19:1–4; 20:10–16; 26:1–2; Deuteronomy 10:16–17; 16:18–20; 18:18–22; Proverbs 24:1–9; 23–26; Hebrews 10:1–31).

Those "negations of liberty," e.g., evil actions with damaging or hurtful consequences, have inspired immense discussions about the causes of

IT'S A CONTINUUM

Human behavior, sums of which, have led certain Human Beings to devise "frames of reference," "systems of thought," "ranges of beliefs," "philosophical systems" or "boxes of mental superstition," compelling them to engage in certain specific activities that, in short, climax into "boxing," "grouping," "labeling," or "cornering," self and other Human Beings, within a "little well-packaged mental box," called a "Stereotype."

Why "stereotypes?" From one instance of observation of one individual Person belonging to a certain ethnic group of people, these so-called "social scientists" proceed to "generalize" the apparently observed behavior TO THE WHOLE ETHNIC GROUP! Because those "labelers" can then develop "a settled way of dealing with such people." Such "dealings," of course, usually focus on external appearance or on physical-material things that "labelers" can manipulate, possess, or control, in order to divert attention from the more spiritual assets and moral principles given to us throughout the ages by God, sums of which, have been observed to be working, even within the realms of Human experience, social relationships, and analytical achievements of moral reflection, even within "the limits and boundaries" set by "laws" enacted with our given free will consent.

"Labeling" people into "a stereotype" allows "the labelers" to have control over both the definition of what is "good behavior" as well as control over "the grouping" of such individuals into a "predetermined whole," thus, inducing prejudicial judgment and inciting negative discrimination against such "a people-group," e.g., "the shanty always-drunk poor-Irishmen!"

Those "systems of thought" or "worldviews" climaxing into the formation of "stereotypes," arose either through some esoteric or biased interpretations of observations of Human behavior; through reflecting and thinking about such Human experiences from which conclusions are wrongly "generalized" or deductions are falsely drawn; or about what animals or lower forms of life do, as they "breathe and move in the jungle" according to their preset deterministic instinctual programming or genetic imprinting, e.g., the theory of evolution; Pavlovian conditioning; Skinnerian behaviorism or operant conditioning; Existentialism; Marxist-Socialism or State-controlled communism, etc...

"Stereotype-producing thought-systems" are contrived in order to arrive at an apparently orderly, well-packaged "frame of expectations," regarding how certain individuals belonging to specific people-groups will "behave" or "how such people-groups ought to act," either under certain experimental conditions or during actual experiential circumstances.

HOW DO WE USE OUR FREE WILL?

Sometimes, such "stereotypic expectations" are formed according to an "opinion poll," from whose procedures and methods, participants' responses, and analyses of results, are "extracted," certain conclusions by "the researchers" or "poll takers," as they frame their biased perceptions within certain "apparently observed patterns of behavior" prevailing in Individual Persons belonging to "certain people-groups" that are then "generalized" as characteristics of said whole people-groups!

However, usually, "the sample size" or "number of participants" is not "statistically valid" due to "wide margins of error" arising from invalid parameters, inconsistent indicators, or unaccounted for extraneous variables, that, hence, render results irrelevant, dubious, scurrilous, and/or inaccurate, sum of which, amounting to "finding out which way the wind is blowing."

The World, as we've come to know it, is full of such "stereotype-producing worldviews:" "The theory of evolution," "socio-biology," "behaviorism," "operant conditioning," or some other "thought-systems" designed for "cultural brain-washing" or "social conditioning:" Such that, in the end, such "thought systems" result in "configuring a set of framed expectations" to emerge or arise from certain groups of people, which, in a nutshell, can be plainly or falsely called, "the Human condition;" and to which, we, sometimes, regrettably and humbly refer, as: "Human Civilization." But God has made another way!

Are Human Beings created or designed "to behave as systematically labeled?" Should "social scientists" develop such "labeling Systems" that box people-groups into individual stereotypes?

Jesus came to teach us differently by giving us "a new commandment:" That we love one another as God loves us, as Christ loves us, as we "see each other through God's eyes," as empowered by His Holy Spirit. (Matthew 22:36–40; 28:18–20; Mark 9:41–42; Luke 6:35–36; John 13:34–35; 15:10–13).

For, Humans are "Spirit-Beings" indwelling an albeit mortal biological body on a temporary basis, whose ultimate "predestined glorification" is to reign together, with Christ Jesus, King of kings and Lord of lords, "in the world to come," as we sit with Him, at "the right hand of power of God."

The Human Mind is built for orderly organization, or for "putting things in order" when "taught properly," inasmuch as it is also prone, to "destructive mentational activities," or for "having bad ideas."

IT'S A CONTINUUM

It is in our Human nature to want to "organize things" into a nice little package, because that simplifies the ways in which we relate to such "packaged things," e.g., As animals are "grouped into Species," Humans are "categorized by race."

From that same vantage point, "bio-scientists" have "pinned" the following organs according to their apparent functions: The heart pumps oxygenated blood for circulation throughout the whole body; the lungs breathe-inhale Oxygen and exhale Carbon Dioxide and Water; kidneys filter all fluids being digested or metabolized by the Human Organism; the liver detoxifies or "gets rid of all toxins" as the immune system releases antigens to fight infections due to bacteria or viruses, etc. . ., all of which, also building "sets of expectations" in the ways the Human Organism "ought to be working," in association with such "boxing patterns" or "caged Systems" of assembling all things into "organized classes" or "grouped categories." Hence, the much vaunted but "deplorable saying:" "To be living in a gilded cage."

Sadly, this is what "Science" has "done to us!" It classifies and categorizes, boxes and groups, for purposes of experimental control or situational manipulation, which "make things a lot simpler" or "easier to deal with" but also very dangerous to our general welfare and very deleterious to our personal well-being. For, things ought to be "kept in perspective:" What is applicable only to things or lower life-forms should not be transferred or extended in application to Humans who are really Spirit-Beings indwelling albeit mortal bodies but who are created unto "the image and likeness of God" for whom the Son of God, Jesus Christ, paid the price of sin! We were "bought with a price:" The precious blood of Jesus Christ who rose from the dead to endow us with "a spirit of power, love, and sound mind." (1 Corinthians 6:15–20; Galatians 2:15–21; 2 Timothy 1:6–8).

Thus, our capacity for "extracting abstraction" from observed natural phenomena or from interpreted social behavior, is sometimes said, to be "both a blessing and a curse." But we are entreated by our loving Creator to judge righteously, not according to appearance, but according to the heart. (Deuteronomy 1:16–17; 1 Samuel 16:6–7; John 7:18–24; Romans 2:1–11).

Some amongst us call this "capacity for abstracting," simply, "imagination." They conclude, then, that it is because of our "imagination," that we are "set apart" from the rest of Nature.

But, in feats of voluntary self-deprecation, it is also even falsely believed, that, because Human Beings "biologically descended from ancestral

HOW DO WE USE OUR FREE WILL?

apes," so say "Evolutionists," that "extensive research" has demonstrated that apes can be "conditioned" to respond to certain stimuli through endless repetitions, such as, "learn sign language," which would then allow them to "communicate" with "the experimenter." It's as if such socio-biologists wish Humanity's suicide so that Apes can prevail in "evolving" into some other "intelligent Species." Of course, that's "wishful thinking."

But, as we all know, to put things "in the realm of Reality," no ape could ever arrive at "imagining," or "extracting from Nature," such an abstraction as, the equation: $E = mc^2$; nor could one chimpanzee ever have the capability to design and construct a spaceship to take it, or us, to the Moon!

God's Word proclaims He created us "unto His own image and likeness." And Christ Jesus, the Son of God, came to live as God amongst Humans to prove God's immense and unfathomable love for us. (Genesis 1:26–27; John 3:16; 17:3; 2 Corinthians 3:17–18; 5:16–17; Colossians 1:11–20; 1 Thessalonians 1:9–10.)

Some "philosophers" would "reason" or "contend," that it is only a matter of "degree," when speaking of "intelligence" or "imagination," when they compare us, Human Beings, to lower forms of life, such as the apes.

There are, biologically speaking, similar operations that might yield "awareness" or "consciousness," some of which, proceeding from "genetically wired traits," or from so-called, "instinctual characteristics," or "brainstem functions," such as the innate needs to eat, to blink the eyes, to breathe, or to sleep.

But these "genetically wired characteristics" cannot be "classified" as "self-conscious free-choice mental intelligence."

However, analyzing one's own thoughts and ideated mental functions, is purely "a Human activity." Apes do not "philosophize" about life and death, right and wrong, or good and evil!

Nor can they be said to be self-aware of their own mortality, like, "in actuarial tables," Human Beings in the United States, are expected to live "a median number of years," such as up to "75 years of age," otherwise called "life expectancy."

Lower forms of life, or animals, "only breathe, move and do, as genetically wired." Honey Bees will "make honey," continuously; or as some people exclaim: "until hell freezes over," which means, always, because Hell can never "freeze over."

It would be "really stretching it to the max" to declare this activity, i.e., "making honey," as an indication of a "form of intelligence" of the same

IT'S A CONTINUUM

kind as that of Human Beings, but different from Human intelligence, only in "degree."

The amoeba is capable of moving from one place to another and of reproducing its own kind, as Human Beings are; but that cannot be classified or categorized as a "form of intelligence."

Immutable genetic characteristics or instinctually wired attributes cannot be called "intelligence." Hence, the fallacy of contriving the much defunct notion of "racial intelligence." For, given the same opportunities for success or prosperity, some individuals of every ethnic group might succeed while other individuals in that same ethnic group might fail! We are not adept at forecasting the future or at predicting the future! Thus, "How a person turns out in life" is such a "complex paradox" that only the Lord knows in advance the actual outcome that will result! For the Lord God, Creator of all things, "knows the end from the beginning!" (Isaiah 45:9–13: 46:8–11).

Thus, in that context, Human Beings can be reflectively conclusive in stating that we do have Liberty to enjoy our God-given freedoms, within their respective limits and boundaries; whereas apes and other animals do not possess such characteristics or traits of being able to act, out of free will, such as "change their views" on certain matters touching their "instinctual existence" — animals act only "on instincts" for a "genetically pre-wired repertoire" of "movement-task-motion performance," in predetermined responses to certain stimuli, respectively, e.g., Honey bees will always collect nectar from flowers and plants "to ultimately make honey!"

Hence, why even wild animals, such as tigers and lions, believed to have been "well-domesticated," might turn against their "handlers" to cause them irreparable injuries or even death.

But, we, Human Beings, can decide that we'll act lovingly towards each other as we pursue the good, do justice, seek peace, and walk humbly before God. (Psalms 34:11–14; Micah 6:8; 1 John 3:4–8; 4:7–21.)

***

HUMAN HISTORY FROM THE VIEWPOINT OF A MORTAL!

So, "what's the alternative?" Is there a "solution" to "the Human condition?" How do we conduct ourselves and guide our temporary lives on the Earth and in the Universe? Why does that matter so much to us all? Which road will we choose during our transient journey on the Earth? The narrow gate that leads to salvation or the wide gate leading to perdition? (Matthew 7:13–14).

We've established thus far that we have God-given Liberty that makes us free, because, Jesus, who delivered us from evil and Hell, is "the Way, the Truth and the Life;" but that we are naturally and spiritually flawed, due to our "inherited mortality" as well due the Laws of Biological Thermodynamics whereby Entropy is ubiquitously spread-out in every natural process, physiological event, or ecological phenomenon; that we are capable of good but also of evil; that, in spite of knowing God's commandments against evil and in spite of all the "laws" we enact consistent therewith, we still "fall short of the mark;" we still falter; we still sin; we still err; but that "God is just and faithful to forgive us our sins when we confess our sins" (Romans 6:20–23; 8:1–17; 1 John 1:9).

Our Creator is so gracious and loving as to allow us to utilize the things He has created for us in order that we might "have a way of life." But, "We can't take anything with us" when we pass away: "No U-haul behind a hearse."

But still, our lives are a precious gift from God, our loving Creator, who "made a way" for us to escape from going to Hell; by simply confessing our sins and commit our faith in Jesus Christ as Lord and Savior; for eternal punishment and banishment from God's righteous presence awaits us after biological death, due to deliberate mortal sins, wrongs, evil, trespasses,

IT'S A CONTINUUM

iniquities, and transgressions against Him for which we have not repented nor sought forgiveness. (2 Corinthians 5:9-11).

We, Human Beings, are not mortal bodies that had to "seek out a soul" or that had to "look for a spirit." To the contrary, we are "living souls," because God Himself had put "the breath of life" in us. We are originally Spirit-Beings temporarily residing "within a biological container," which we call: our Human Organism.

And, as we are reckoning with this Reality: That we are "Spirit-Beings" who are temporarily indwelling our mortal bodies, then we patiently await the time or "divine appointment" when we will then return to the original Source from whence we came. (Ephesians 3:7-21; Hebrews 2:9-18). So, as intimated above, We're "just passing through!"

Satan was a spirit also, but, an angel who was cast down to "the lower parts of the heaven," due to his rebellion against God's heavenly and earthly dominion (Isaiah 14:12-20; 28:14-19; Ezekiel 28:1-19).

For the Holy Bible tells us that Satan "took the form of a Serpent" in the Garden of Eden. As an angel who rebelled against God in his attempt to usurp God's sovereign authority in Heaven and on Earth, Satan, otherwise called Lucifer, or "false light," — because Jesus is the true real "Light of the world" — attempted to dethrone God's "eternal suzerainty" and "everlasting dominion" over all things created, and over all things that exist! (Psalms 1:5-6; 24:1-2; 110:1:1, Corinthians 15:20-28).

Having lost his place as "a princely cherub," Satan could no longer challenge God's sovereignty in "spirit form;" so, he sought to "invade" or "possess" the living bodies of Human Beings whom he would deceive into performing works of evil that would desecrate "God's image and likeness" in us, as we forgo the leadership of Christ as the supreme authority in our lives, to then accept Satan's as a substitute authority.

But Satan is a "defeated foe" who has no original power, and hence, why he is steeped in deceitful machinations that lead us astray so that we forget "who we are in Christ" to then fall into perpetrating evil wickedness, at times against the legitimate interests of others, and often, against our own best interests. (Romans 16:19-20; 1 Corinthians 15:58; 2 Corinthians 2:10-11; James 1:22-25; 1 John 3:4-10).

Satan, Lucifer the "false light," "the usurper" also wants "to supplant" our Christ-likeness with his evil schemes and wicked designs, in order to "transmogrify" our character into "his image and likeness" or into "the image of the beast," so that his evil machinations might "prosper" in the heavenly realm as well as on the Earth rather than God's genuine goodness and loving kindness in Christ Jesus. (Genesis 3:15; 2 Corinthians 11:12–15; Ephesians 6:10–12; 13–20; Revelation 13:11–18).

God's Living Word of Truth has been revealed to us by His Holy Spirit through Christ Jesus our Lord to set us free permanently once and for all from "all the deceitful winds of doctrine" that are contrived by Satan and his followers on the Earth.

Jesus is "the seed of Abraham," "father of faith," who mirrored true faith in God, through the attempted sacrifice of Isaac, his "son of promise." God did not let that happen because He was only "testing Abraham's obedience," so as to seal, for us, once and for all, our Salvation in "a covenant of faith," through "prefiguring" Christ's sacrificial death on the Cross as atonement and propitiation for the redemption of our sins. (Genesis 21:12; Hebrews 11:17–22).

The Holy Bible reveals that every family on the Earth obtains its name from the heavenly realm from which we had already been conceived in the mind and heart of God, our loving Heavenly Father. That, through our faith, Christ Jesus, and we, share the same blessed "spiritual conception," because, at first, we originated from the same heavenly Source, Almighty God, from whom Christ came as "the way, the truth and the life," and with whom we are "heirs" to God's kingdom and inheritors of eternal life.

Christ, "the Seed of Abraham's faith," — "Abraham believed God and it was reckoned to him as righteousness," — in the likeness of Abraham also believed God by His faithful obedience of God's Will for His earthly and heavenly life as revealed by His prayers in the Garden of Gethsemane, — who was entombed within the bowels of the Earth, rose from the dead, so that in Him, we have "life more abundant" and Eternal Life! Christ's righteousness becomes our righteousness, in the likeness of Abraham's believing God, "credited to him as righteousness," through his faithful obedience of God's Will. (Genesis 15:6; John 8:31–32; 9:5; 14:6–7; Romans 4:3; Galatians 3:6; Ephesians 3:14–19; Hebrews 2:10–18; James 2:23).

Jesus is "the Word of God made flesh." God spoke the Universe, the Earth and us into being through His spoken word: "Let there be light, and there was light; and the Lord saw that the light was good."

Jesus was also present at the time of Creation, as He is the Son of God, "Elohim," who said, "Let us make man in our own image and likeness." (Genesis 1:26–27).

IT'S A CONTINUUM

Jesus is the "light of men" who gives us the Truth that sets us free; and "the light of the world" who dissipates and casts out the evil darkness of Satan's wicked designs. (John 1:1–5; 3:19; 8:12; 9:5).

Thus, as free spirit-beings indwelling a mortal temporary biological body on this Planet, we have the choice to decide "which road we will take," "which path we will follow," or "which gate" we will enter: "The narrow gate" leads to life; "the wide gate" leads to death. (Matthew 7:13–16; 20; John 8:31–36; 10:7–18; 14:1–7; Acts 4:12).

We can decide to either be "slaves of evil," in bondage to the ways of death or the ways of Cain, as suborned under the devil, who, by his deceitful wiles, murdered his own brother, Abel; to live miserably, without hope in the world, "tossed to and fro by every wind of doctrine," churning on how to get revenge on our neighbors for wrongs they transgressed against us; while being addicted to toxic emotions from wicked thoughts or evil ideas our minds are feeding on; and doing the Devil's works on the Earth, which "legitimize the false authority of Satan," that defeated foe and hideous author of sin; OR, we can become "servants of righteousness," "children of light," through Christ, as we are living in the "glorious liberty of the children of God" that God bestowed upon us through Christ, which gives us the opportunity to do what is right and good on the Earth, not only for our own interests but also for he interests of others, sum of which, gives due glory, power, dominion, authority, and honor to God our heavenly Father. (Matthew 5:48; Matthew 22:26–40; Galatians 5:13–15; Philippians 2:1–11).

Jesus Christ rose from the dead and death was "swallowed up in victory!" (1 Corinthians 15:51–58; 1 John 5:1–12).

Thus, as diligent followers and faithful servants of Christ, we either glorify God by our good deeds towards each other on the Earth; or we choose to demean, mock, and deride "God's image and likeness" in us. For God imparted to us His "character-traits" or "character-qualities" that set us apart from all the rest of Creation. (John 8:31–36; Romans 6:12–14; 17–19; 14:16–19; Galatians 2:18–20).

Through "God-denying belief systems," like "the theory of evolution," and wrongful actions, such as lawless violence that displaces God's sovereign authority to guide and instruct us unto His peace by "the way we ought to live," many wicked and faithless people elevate "the image of the beast," as lured into "the chains of bondage," and reflecting "the likeness of Satan," by their "appreciation and valuation," of evil, as contrived by the Devil, who was, from the beginning a murderer, a liar and a thief that has come to

HUMAN HISTORY FROM THE VIEWPOINT OF A MORTAL!

steal, kill, and destroy. But Jesus blesses us with the truth that sets us free for enjoyment of "life more abundant," and also everlasting life. (Psalms 14:1; 53:1; John 8:42–47; 10:7–18; Romans 6:5–19).

Therefore, our faith in God matters! We are spirit-beings who can't escape, neither from the knowledge of good and evil, nor from God's commandments to do what is right. (1 Corinthians 8:1–3; 14:33; 15:32–34; 49–58; 16:13; 2 Corinthians 2:10–11).

Yet, Sinfulness and Entropy, subduing the flesh unto perdition, plague us with fault and failure. But God freed us from the grip of the Devil's dominion. Thus, "we have passed from death unto life" through Christ, the Son of the living God. (John 5:24; Colossians 1:11–14; 1 John 3:14).

What is a "nation?" A nation is an assembly, a union, a congregation of peace-seeking and peace-making "neighborly families" made-up of individual-citizen Persons, who together, are "transformed" or "made new," by God's Spirit in Christ, to "live free in the bond of Love." (Ephesians 4:1–8).

The Church is "the body of Christ." As the body has many parts that fulfill diverse necessary functions, so are we all, members of the same Body. (Romans 2:6–11; 1 Corinthians 12:7; 20–26; Galatians 5:5–6).

We, all, in society," from the diaper to the coffin," depend and rely upon each other's good works, in order to "live well," or in order to enjoy, "the more abundant life," according to God's plan of Salvation for us, in fulfillment of His sure promise of eternal life to us. (John 3:16; John 17:3; Ephesians 3:1–13).

Are we not injured or harmed by each other's wicked works of evil that give false honor to Satan's corrupt spiritual nature and deceitful underhanded ways of bondage and death? Surely, must not our faith in God correspond to our good deeds? "For as the body without the spirit is dead, faith without works is dead." (James 2:26; 4:6–8; Ephesians 5:1–14).

We are already mortal in this temporary biological body; and die, we will, eventually. So why pursue lawless violence and cruelty by doing evil things that accelerate or prematurely bring about, such, as our suffering, tribulation, or death? (1 Corinthians 10:12–13; 12:7; 16:13; 2 Corinthians 5:7; 2 Corinthians 10:1–17).

Because of our sinful Human nature and because of Entropy, we'll end up dying anyway, eventually, for an honorable burial in the cemetery of our choice. (Hebrews 9:27–28; 10:1–3; 12:1–2).

Given that evil works on the Earth do NOT bring us "Biological Immortality" by whose urgings covetous people crave and covet unjust

IT'S A CONTINUUM

corrupt powers because of "the lusts of the flesh, the lusts of the eyes, and the pride of life," we can freely make the deliberate spiritual choice to follow the moral principles handed down to us from Christ, by the Prophets and the Apostles, and other faithful disciples of Jesus Christ. (Ephesians 3:1–13; Titus 2:11–15; 3:4–8; 1 Peter 2:25).

For our Lord and Savior, Jesus, is the ultimate necessary original end-in-view or supremely promised imperative climax of all Human History! From the very first steps in our beginnings, we were in dire need of a Savior. (Genesis 3:15; John 3:16; 1 Corinthians 3:10–11; Colossians 1:11–20; 2:15–19).

Which "thought system," worldview," "belief system" or "philosophy" contrived by the Human mind has resulted in our ultimate biological immortality? None! Not one!

Which of these, has yielded a course of limitless extension of our temporary lives on the Earth? None. Not one!

Which "philosophy of life" has brought to us "all the good things" that "flesh-and-blood" craves, covets, lusts after, and seeks after, and pursues? None! No, not one!

Except that such Humanly-contrived doctrines pretending to suffice in fulfilling our deepest innate needs for love, compassion, friendship, peace, goodness, kindness, freedom, and justice, only induce and seduce us "to arrogate unto ourselves" the wicked fruits or evil designs brought into being in our hearts, born from "the lusts of the flesh, the lusts of the eyes, and the pride of life." (1 John 2:15–17; 2 John 1:7–9).

"Human philosophies," apart from God's wisdom, are always fruitless, futile, useless, and vain. (Romans 1:16–32, KJV).

"Philosophies" contrived by godless evolutionists, always turn out that such "esoteric masking of evil intentions" will result in being a "conspiratorial narrative" that lures and entraps "followers," but only for corruptly benefiting or giving unjust advantages only to its authors and their "close circle of friends;" that is, only for a short time, until, by the grace of God, they are defeated through the Holy Spirit in Christ our Lord and Savior; or until they, those so-called "philosophers" and their "followers" themselves, pass away, e.g., ensuing from the violent unjust system of thought gaining currency out of the theory of evolution; from Marxist-Socialism whereby festers a fascist dictatorship of the masses of people by an elite that takes control of the State's government, the country's industries, and the nation's military forces, e.g., Hitler, Mussolini, Stalin, etc . . .

HUMAN HISTORY FROM THE VIEWPOINT OF A MORTAL!

Human philosophies, — whether Marxist Communism, State-controlled Socialism, Evolutionist Socio-Biology, or Existentialism, to name just a few, — end up being "narratives of disasters," or "plans for Human self-extinction," or "plots for national suicide" that revolve in a "convoluted and confounding cycle of flawed reasoning," which eventually culminates and climaxes into a dead-end, e.g., Racial or ethnic mythologies that promote: Warfare, conquests of land; slave-making; thieveries; plunder and pillage for "spoils, loot, and booty," etc . . . ; or the so-called "dictatorship of the proletariat" professed by Marxist-Socialism pontificating that every stage of economic development, from mercantilism to Capitalism, contains "the seeds of its own destruction," but yet, concocts "a convenient exemption" from such contradictions for "the State" that will simply "wither away."

Why would "the Marxist-Socialist State wither away" when it is the most confounding unitary engine of so many convoluted contradictions, especially in acquisitions of power, access to influence-peddling, and distribution of wealth? Given "the Human Condition," Why would it not also contain "the seeds of its own destruction" when all forms of unchecked powers are so compressed and concentrated into the same fewer hands? Figures! There is "something very fishy" with this type of deceitful macabre contradictory reasoning! "The logic" just does not stand up to sense-making scrutiny by any measure of probity, clarity, honesty, or integrity!

Marxist-Socialist socio-political economic philosophy "stops dead in its own tracks!" For "the State" becomes "frozen in time," ossified in wielding despotic power, and petrified in perpetrating cruel injustices in order to perpetuate its own monstrous fascist legacy!

Therefore, by way of Marxist-Socialist doctrinal principles, "the State," never "withers away!" To the contrary, given what we know regarding Human Nature's sinfulness and natural physical environmental and biological Entropy plaguing "our Human Condition," "the State," godless, secular, flesh-centered, and humanist, becomes even more entrenched, more despotic, more clannish, and more cruel in perpetrating the vilest forms of injustices, "than at any previous stage of economic development."

Such godless philosophies are dead-ended mythologies resulting in "historical catastrophes" because their "authors and creators," are themselves also flawed, error-prone, sinful, self-serving, egocentric, clannish, because of Human spiritual-moral sinfulness and biological-physiological Entropy, and, of course, eventual death. (Galatians 3:15–20; 4:1–11; 5:1–19;

IT'S A CONTINUUM

1 Timothy 1:8–11; 4:1–10; 16; 5:20–21; 6:14–21; 2 Timothy 1:8–10;13; 2:8–13;15; 23–25; 3:1–9; 4:3–4; 17–18).

The "Marxist-Socialist State" then becomes the most gruesome epitome of national suicidal fascism ever devised by the Human mind. For, Mortal Humans cannot originally initiate or create any thing whose continuous operations must rest on their flawed temporary lives. So, there can be no such thing as "a perpetual machine." Eternal things are created by God who can neither lie nor die. Hence, the truthfulness and veracity of our Creator's Word of love and peace in Christ Jesus our Lord! (Numbers 23:19; John 17:3; Hebrews 8:13; 13:8; Colossians 3:15–17).

Unanswered questions, perplexing dilemmas, obsolete or defunct plans, confounding reasoning, and/or contradictory statements would persist and plague the flawed, dead-ended, "Marxist-Socialist logic," sum of which, negating both adherents' worldview and the supposed "good results," that were to ensue from "followers" taking hold of their convoluted creeds that have no basis in self-evident Truths that are confirmed by well-known historical Human experience.

God Himself is a Spirit and cannot lie, nor die. God's only "self-interest" is His unfathomable redemptive love for us! God had sent His only begotten Son, Jesus Christ, to die on the Cross in our place, after which, He rose from the dead to empower us with "righteous living" on the Earth and "life eternal" thereafter. Thus, Immortality craved; cravings fulfilled! Life in the Spirit of Christ promotes the well-being of all and secures the welfare of all. Goodness is ensured for our earthly living and eternal life awaits us thereafter — a "win-win situation." (John 3:16; 17:3; Galatians 2:18–21; Colossians 3:1–11; 12–13; 4:5–6).

Self-centered egotistic megalomaniacal selfishness recedes in the background of Human thinking, experience, and behavior, as our real needs and truly innate beneficent desires, are fulfilled for all, because this "more abundant life" we receive from communing with Christ through God's Holy Spirit, brings us love, peace, liberty, justice, charity, forbearance, patience, and prosperity. (John 17:14–19; Romans 8:26–30; Galatians 3:1–14).

Christ's resurrection from the dead not only sealed, once and for all, our justification and sanctification, and the demise of Satan's evil schemes, wicked thoughts, and wicked ways, but it also secures our atonement and redemption from destructive sins and fatal choices, as well as permanently safeguards our exculpation, and thus, our exemption from the fires of Hell! (2 Corinthians 1:21–22; Ephesians 1:13–14).

Through the power of Christ's resurrection from the dead, God "made a way" for us to freely repent of our sins in order to graciously and mercifully obtain forgiveness that then frees us for beginning anew (2 Timothy 1:7; 1 John 1:9).

For since the crime of Cain against his brother Abel, through the sinful kings who misled "the children of Israel," God's plan had been unfolding with a "saved Remnant," in accordance with His Word of Truth and Love through the Prophets. Humans have been pursuing "a return to paradise" ever since, through "the law" as a "custodian" or "constrainer," or "taskmaster," until "grace and truth came through Jesus Christ." (John 1:1–18; Romans 7:4–6; Hebrews 10:26–31).

Because "the law," though good, is powerless in restraining the irrational lusts of the flesh, only through the love of Christ are there Peace and Justice in the world, as well as eternal life thereafter. (Psalms 24:1; 127:1–3; Isaiah 66:1; Romans 8:35–39).

For "the pride of life" that caters to carnal desires and thoughtless wants pursuing "spiritual satisfaction" and "emotional fulfillment" from material possessions, will foster hatred, hostility, wars of revenge instead of repentance from transgressions and forgiveness of trespasses; and/or fights and battles for conquests of land and natural resources, the brunt of which, destroying the social assets and tearing-up the cultural fabric that keep a nation free and just, peaceful and prosperous, purposeful and democratic. But, as the sacred Scriptures tell us: We are the temple for God's Holy Spirit through the risen Christ whose love indwells us. (1 Corinthians 3:16–20; 6:13–20; 2 Corinthians 6:14–18.)

Is a man devoted to wickedness "immortal?" Committing evil does not increase our lifespan! Perpetrating wrongs against our neighbors does not result in giving us Immortality! But doing good towards one another in love and peace brings justice to our freedoms that we exercise and enjoy by the Grace of God. "Overcoming evil with good," is not only rewarding in and of itself, but may, ultimately, extend the duration of our living existence on the Earth, barring unforeseeable accidents and natural disasters, and barring destructive choices that shorten the length of our earthly journey, e.g., NOT engaging in illicit drug addictions and perverted sexual activities, will prevent us from contracting harmful illnesses, fatal diseases, and premature death through exchange of needles or "passing" of bodily fluids. (Romans 1:26–32; 1 Timothy 3:15–16).

Such as above-described destructive behaviors shorten the duration of Human life which is so precious as an indescribable gift and inexpressible endowment from our Creator that allow us to enjoy, not only "the blessings of liberty to ourselves and our posterity," but also to secure a well-earnestly gained legacy of which we are not ashamed and that leaves no regrets, no remorse, and no resentment, because of a clear conscience. (Acts 23:1; 24:14–16; 2 Corinthians 1:12; 4:2; 13:8; Hebrews 13:18; 1 Timothy 1:19; 3:9; 2 Timothy 1:3).

So, given that vain Human philosophies, worldviews, thought systems, belief systems, and ways of Human-focused thinking that are ungodly bring us injustice, enmity, hostility, war, bondage, injuries, harm, and even premature death without also giving us that which we covet and crave: Immortality: Then where are we to turn?

If immortality in the flesh is what most godless men reluctantly crave and desperately lust after, — and they can't obtain that which they cringingly or fearfully covet, — then, why do they concoct "substitutes" into which to "invest their energies" so as to alleviate the "cognitive dissonance" and the contradictions raging in their conscience, e.g., through the pursuit of wealth due to love of money from which to extract "fame and power in the world," of which, "Satan is the prince?" "Substitute investments" of worldly energies "don't work either" — We remain as mortal as we were before, but more miserable, the more hungry for genuine love, starving for true fellowship with God, and the more vulnerable to Satan's enticements, lures, baits, and entrapments! The whisky bottle then appears to have "a strange," even irresistible attraction!" Illicit drugs ingested as "precursors of violence" operate to sabotage our relationships and demean God's character-qualities in our inner-being. We need help from Jesus whose love for us never fails to uplift our spirits and cleanse our souls from despair, hopelessness, apathy, resignation, and indifference.

"Secular Humanism" is a "dead-ended religion," worldview, and philosophy that only bring violence, destruction, war, lawlessness, anarchy, and death!

For, absent God's Holy Spirit to guide us unto which "laws, ordinances, statutes, policies or rules" best be legislated, and to instruct us on how "laws" are to be applied in a just and fair manner, Humans succumb to excesses that propel us "beyond the civilized norms, limits and boundaries" so long pursued in order to keep us in Liberty, sum of which, resulting in cruelty, injustice, oppression, slavery, bondage, self-destruction, and premature death.

As Lord Acton is said to have put it: "Power corrupts; and absolute power corrupts absolutely."

For, due to our innate sinful nature, we, Humans, are "intrinsically lawless" and "inherently selfish" from the start of our infancy, so as to be despoiled of all the wherewithal that makes for "civilized living." Hence why Scriptures tell us:

"Train up a child in the way he should go, and when he is old he will not depart from it." (Proverbs 1:7; 8:13; 22:6–8).

Satan is also aware of this remarkable process, hence, why his wicked followers try to "hijack" a nation's educational system in order to corrupt Humans from infancy and youth upwards, from which deescalate, as an engulfing avalanche, all the troubles, tribulations, dangers, and threats that "Man represents for Man."

Thus, from infanticide to euthanasia, from prostitution to sodomy and lesbianism, from illicit drug legalization to "addictive pseudo-functioning," Eric Fromm's so-called "Man for himself," or Nietzsche's "Super-Human" or so-called "Ubermensch," has proven to be a formula for national suicide, cultural self-destruction, and Human self-extinction.

It is often said that repeating the same actions or performing the same activities while expecting a different result from that previously obtained, is "a form of insanity," or rather, of "senseless absurdity."

In fact, some Human Beings, e.g., atheists, evolutionists, and existentialists, hold the belief that Human existence is "a theater of the absurd;" that there is no meaningful purpose to life on the Earth; and that all the things we see, perceive, know, and understand "only came into being by chance accident" due to "random probability." Like all lower forms of life, or animals: we're born; we live; we drop dead! But, God forbid!

Such worldviews bring only wicked thinking and evil actions that lead to injuries, harm, and or premature death — because such negative obsessions bring us to say, "What's the point?" "Only live for today for tomorrow we die!" Those "philosophers" are not only committing suicide, "by all measures of reasoning," but might regrettably fancy or fantasize that "they also have the option" to take others with them to their own self-inflicted doom. (Psalms 14:1; 53:1–3; Isaiah 22:12–14; 1 Corinthians 15:32–34).

IT'S A CONTINUUM

We do have free will to choose any course of action, prudently and safely, justly and peaceably, lawfully and fairly, within the limits of natural laws of Entropy, as well as within the "boundaries" of the socio-economic political laws to which we agree to consent in society for our own good and for the good of our neighbors; for the good of society as a whole, and for the good of the "ecological environment," from all of which, we breathe, drink, eat, labor, create, invent, produce, utilize, and prosper.

However, "pursuit of immortality" in flesh-and-blood, — or substitute obsessions amounting to "Obsessive Compulsive Disorders" — devised by the Human mind in order to "cope with this non-reality," or "adapt to" that impracticality and falsehood, called, immortality, or in order to escape from the anxieties, discomfort, and dissonance that this "vexing paradox" engenders, — To be able to "do all this" and then drop dead to leave it all behind — is an "impossible objective" in this "world of sinfulness and Entropy;" but "the life to come," that is, eternal life, (John 3:16; John 17:3) has been given to us through our faith in Christ, which, is also "the victory that overcomes the world." (1 John 5:1–5).

Evolutionists cannot ever "adapt" to death! It's a final, terminal biological ending! Satan is "the prince of this world" which is in bondage to confusion, deception, violence addictions, lawlessness, and death, whereas Christ is "the prince of peace." (Isaiah 9:6–7; John 6:27; 16:7–11; Corinthians 14:33).

Satan's evil and wicked spirit exploits "our struggles and strivings" for what we are "living to defeat" every day of our lives: Sin and Entropy!

But we can't do it alone! Jesus has already made a way for us to be victorious over the Devil and his deceitful schemes. (Romans 16:19–20; 1 Corinthians 10:13; 2 Corinthians 2:10–11; Philippians 4:4–13; 1 Peter 2:16–17; 1 John 3:4–8; 5:18–21).

Vicissitudes of Human nature, or our Human frailties that result in perpetrated wrongs and perpetuating violence and injustice, appeal to the Devil's deadly desires to lure and entrap us unawares into its demonic schemes concocted in order "to steal, kill and destroy," which in the end induce despair, hopelessness, apathy, indifference, and resignation. (John 10:7-18; 2 Corinthians 2:10–11; 1 Peter 5:6–11).

But God's Spirit erects a barrier against Satan's availing himself of numerous opportunities to seduce us into succumbing to committing evil acts from a wicked heart and a hostile mind. (1 Corinthians 10:12–13; 12:26).

HUMAN HISTORY FROM THE VIEWPOINT OF A MORTAL!

For Jesus is "the way, the truth and the life," and no one comes to God, enters His throne of Mercy, or pleads innocence at His altar of grace, to our heavenly Father, but only through Jesus Christ who shed His holy blood as a propitiation that atones for our sins." (John 14:6–7).

Salvation is in no one else! Salvation is a free gift from God's grace so that no flesh can boast through works and deeds. (Acts 4:8–12; Ephesians 2:8–10).

We receive forgiveness for our sins only through the shed blood of Jesus on the Cross and are thereafter empowered for good works of faith by His resurrection from the dead and ascension unto Heaven. When we accept the sacrifice of Christ as atonement for our sins, because He rose from the dead, His Holy Spirit, through communication and communion, attends to our inner-needs that have to be fulfilled in the right way in order that we might enjoy "the more abundant life" as we're "only passing through" on the Earth, and that we might receive Life Eternal thereafter.

"There is no U-haul behind a hearse!" And "the monkey with the most toys" wins nothing — such persons regrettably and fatefully entertaining that they "descended from the apes," leave every thing behind. So, what's the point of pursuing evil, violence, injustice, and conquest? Why accelerate the inevitable! God forbid!

We came into this world as naked little babies needing diapers and clothing, and return to the dust of the ground of the Earth from whence we came biologically, in like manner, naked, and needing garments, clothing, or "a covering," so to speak, for our biological bodies, laying in a coffin that is to be buried honorably in the cemetery of our choice.

The Word of God in the Holy Bible tells us that "love covers a multitude of sins." (James 5:19–20).

Only Christ gives us "a covering of justification" that purifies our hearts and cleanses our conscience before the Judgment Seat of God. (2 Corinthians 5:10; 1 Peter 2:16).

Thus, with the joy of the Lord in our hearts, we can rejoice as we are empowered to rebuke Satan, crush his head under our feet, resist his lies and deceptions, and destroy his wicked evil works on the Earth and "in the spirit realm." (Romans 16:19–20; Ephesians 6:10–20; Philippians 4:4–13; James 4:4–10).

Through repentance and forgiveness, we are empowered again with our restored God-given liberty in order to do what is right in His eyes, for our own benefit and for the interest of others, no longer in bondage to evil

IT'S A CONTINUUM

wickedness that brings us grief, pain, suffering, tribulation, travails, and even, ultimately, premature death. (Philippians 2:1–11).

Freedom is the God-given power to use one's own Liberty to do what is right, good, and pleasing to God. "Happiness" is transient because it is "situational." But "Joy" is eternal because it comes from the Spirit of God in Christ Jesus who loves us beyond words can express. Love and peace give us joy that enlightens our deepest hopes. (Psalms 90:14; John 3:16; 5:24; 15:9–13; 16:23–25; 31–33; 17:1–3; Romans 15:13; 1 John 1:1–4; 2 John 1:12; Revelation 21:1–4; 22:3–5).

For as we are inspired, instructed, persuaded, convicted, convinced, and judged, as a just and holy commandment, we freely desire to love God, and to love each other in "peaceful neighborliness," even as we enjoy to love our own selves while engaged in the "pursuit of Happiness," or in the pursuit of what we perceive and understand to be for our own good, benefit, advantage, interest, and/or right.

"Happenstance" might bring "happiness! But the joy of the Lord is eternal life that overcomes earthly obstacles or difficult situations, to rekindle and illuminate Hope in the Will of God for "life more abundant." (John 10:7–13).

We leave it all behind and thus, there is plenty for us all in this vast Universe! We came into this world as little babies to discover "the world as it is." (Psalms 24:1; 127:1–3; Isaiah 66:1).

We brought nothing into it but God had already prepared every ecological phenomenon in life-support systems that supply fulfillment of our needs. We plant a seed in the soil, and "boom," in due season, comes out a fruit; burst forth "waves of grain!" Our farmers are so extensively and exceedingly productive in agricultural output that our excess grain, e.g., corn, is industrially processed into Ethanol to be added to gasoline!

But, receiving and giving love, practicing charity, and showering Mercy upon one another, are God's divinely cast prescriptions for our capabilities to be "trained in righteousness" in order to overcome evil thoughts, injurious ideas, grievous emotions, and wicked actions that might cause personal harm, injury, or premature death to others.

Don't we keep little children away from hot burners of a cooking stove in order to protect them from being burnt and injured by the extremely high temperatures?

Are we not "grown-ups," or are we "adult little babies" who have matured in age, and presumed to have "learnt about life" with a greater understanding of moral consideration, hospitable generosity, and practical civility? (1 Corinthians 13:11–13)

Have we not "received power from on high," the love of Christ that edifies, up-builds, and uplifts our social relations with the "lubrication" needed to facilitate our mutual transactions without strife, adversity, hostility, grief, or violence?

If the little children to whom God has given life through their parents are safeguarded through listening to their instructions, guidance, direction, and exhortation, then why is it so difficult to accept that our Creator Almighty God can legitimately and mightily and lovingly entreat us unto beneficent thoughts, good ideas, and just deeds? (Galatians 4:8–9; Ephesians 4:15–16).

Isn't it a fact that we continuously learn from each other, either as infants or teen-agers; or either as adults or mature persons? (Galatians 6:6).

Then, what's wrong with freely deciding to engage in learning how to produce righteous works on the Earth through our faith in God, as we are guided by Prophets and Apostles, who wrote the Word of God as inspired by His Holy Spirit in Christ Jesus? (Proverbs 8:13; 14:34; 22:6; Galatians 6:6; 2 Timothy 3:16–17.)

Why does our age make a difference in "the equation of teaching-and-learning" how to do what is right and good for ourselves and our neighbors? (1 Corinthians 11:1; 13:11–13; Galatians 4:12; 6:6; 2 Timothy 3:16–17).

Isn't it acquired prideful arrogance in fancying that "we know it all," that "we're right and everyone else is wrong," that we "know what's best for ourselves," even as we are reckoning with our own shortcomings, vices, frailties, faults, errors, mistakes, and vicissitudes? (Romans 6:11–14; 20–23; 7:6; 12:19–21 14:17–19; 1 Corinthians 4:16–18; 5:1–5; 10:12–13; 11:1).

Nevertheless, we do endeavor to "act properly" under parental instructions and teachers' guidance, as "little children" who need direction. But, as "little children," because of "our in-utero ignorance," or "post-natal innocence," — in that, our attitudes, thoughts, and emotions from which emerge our beliefs and actions, have not yet been "stained by the evil world" in which we live, — the Lord is gracious and forbearing to forgive us when we falter. (1 John 1:5–9).

Yet, apart from natural disasters and unforeseen illnesses, diseases, and accidents, that "evil world" consists of us, Human Beings, one another, in relation to each other, as "sabotaged" by Satan who is "the prince of this world."

IT'S A CONTINUUM

Why is there a saying amongst the godless such as: "We have met the enemy and it is us?"

Why must the world be evil — notwithstanding Scriptures stating that Satan is "the prince of this world?" Why can't we mortals utilize our free will to do what we know is right and good for ourselves and our neighbors, or for other people in our social circle of relationships?

The physical flesh craves to possess material things; even to the point of "controlling others" and "manipulating events" for its own irrational passions that feed on its lusts for unjust power and corrupt gain! (Romans 2:27-29; 3:9-20; 8:6-8; 1 John 2:1-5; 15-17; 3:9-18; 4:1-6; 2 John 1:9).

Yes, we have a sinful nature or flawed character; yes, the physical environment and natural phenomena are rife with Entropy.

Still, don't we have numerous opportunities, plans, and goals for living in peace with one another, to prosper together in the same social environment, when we want to collaborate or co-labor, in "building a better world" or "a more perfect Union?" (Matthew 5:43-48).

"In order to form a more perfect Union" or "to secure the blessings of liberty to ourselves and our Posterity" in the Preamble of the Constitution of the United States of America is not written "by accident" or "by random chance." It is deliberately stated and published for the world to know! In 1776, and even in our world, these miraculous hopes and accomplishments are worth co-laboring for!

America's Founders thought it throughout. From their learning from history and Human experience, and divine inspiration, they duly deliberated and freely discussed things concerning "creating a new form of government," before making such momentous pronouncements as mandated principles in our Constitution.

As they, like we, have continuously observed, Human Beings can always improve their circumstances through helping each other out, notwithstanding the negative influences that might be present from sinfulness and Entropy, e.g., Slavery of Black Americans for which our ancestors fought a Civil War from 1861 through 1865, during which time, President Abraham Lincoln was also assassinated!

America's Founders knew of such "civilized social processes" and honestly held the belief that we, also, their posterity, could simultaneously, freely preserve the good they had accomplished, while deliberately engaged in redressing the wrongs that they had inflicted upon others, at the time of the Founding, — e.g., enslavement of Black people and disenfranchisement of women of their right to vote, — through our commitments to "progressively refine" or "systematically fine-tune" how we apply those constitutional principles that nurture our "Life, Liberty and pursuit of Happiness."

Only by "speaking and doing the truth in love," and serving each other with love might we prevail in nourishing justice, peace, and prosperity, even as we are blessed with nurturing repentance that frees us and forgiveness that empowers us: For newness of life, even as we pursue the enjoyment of our inalienable God-endowed gifts, endowments, and rights. (1 Corinthians 15:49–50; Colossians 3:12–17; 2 Timothy 2:19; James 1:16–18; 4:13–17; Hebrews 10:19–25; 2 Peter1:3–11; 1 John 3:7–8; 18).

Have we not applied, by the grace of Almighty God who is forbearing towards us, the above-described socio-political processes for redressing deleterious damages that had flowed from enslaving Afro-Americans and from suppressing their voting rights?

Have we not redressed the cruel injustice of disparaging the voting rights of all American women in our midst?

Today, even eighteen year-olds manning M-16's, grenades, tanks, and bombs in our armed forces can now exercise their voting rights in accordance with an Amendment that consistently aligns with constitutional principles of liberty, truth, tranquility, and justice. (26th Amendment to the Constitution of the United States of America.)

As proven by our analysis then, the "system of free government" that America's Founders passed onto us, and which our Forbears or previous generations had to have improved, works well, but only as we earnestly endeavor to ameliorate our social relations that are dependent upon its "political economy:" With God's grace and Christ's love and forbearance, by finding "the right approach" and discovering "the right processes," for resolving our disputes and problems.

Yes, we can say that "The system works!" however slowly and "imperfectly," still! We are Human, folks! That's no excuse for injuring each other deliberately, but, as long as we are "in this fleshly tent," our flaws will overflow into almost every thing we do. But, as long as we remain a free nation, a representative constitutional democratic republic, "One nation, under God, indivisible, with liberty and justice for all," with the Constitution and our Bill of Rights enshrined as "the supreme Law of the land," then, our pursuit of improvements and ameliorations, through "progressive refinements" of constitutional principles of free government, their fair and just applications to our common predicament, — within the limits, boundaries,

IT'S A CONTINUUM

checks-and-balances, separation of powers, division of powers , public responsibility and accountability; and within the scope of other provisions embedded within "auxiliary precautions" that restrain abuses of government — we can justly, peacefully and lawfully bring to bear, "our citizens' constructive inputs," upon the general welfare of our "social whole" and the well-being of all.

For, as President Lincoln prophesied: "That this nation, under God, shall have a new birth of freedom — and that government of the people, by the people, for the people, shall not perish from the earth." (November 19, 1863, at Gettysburg Cemetery.)

Thus, if we remain faithful to the "progressive refinement" of our applications of the constitutional principles inherent in our form of free government, we are pre-destined to ultimately succeed in advancing the march of improvements and the birth of ameliorations that will get us closer to fulfillment of our constitutionally prescribed mandate: "in order to form a more perfect Union!" But only, by remaining "UNDER GOD!"

***

WHY ONLY JESUS!

BY OUR FAITH THROUGH Christ, our character begins to form, shape, mold, nurture, and nourish our attitudes, sentiments, emotions, capacities to discern and reason, capabilities to think, and commitments to act lovingly, justly, peacefully, and lawfully. We continue to mature throughout our lives unto "the image and likeness of God," our Creator, whom Jesus Christ embodied in-the-flesh by His coming upon the Earth to redeem us from sin and hell.

Then can we continuously increase our well-being, from one level of understanding to another, from one degree of application to another, and from one enjoyment of Happiness to another, in how to live on the Earth, at home and abroad, with other Human Beings: As "a new creation," "born of the Spirit," "born of God!" (2 Corinthians 3:17–18).

"Progressive refinements," through a process that approximates our system of free government, to arrive, "closer and closer," to "a more perfect Union," proceed in justly applying the constitutional principles of free government which we inherited as a forthright legacy, beholding them as a Reality that we need to grasp, understand, comprehend, and take hold of.

Applying "progressive refinements" to constitutional principles of free government, means "fine-tuning" the ways in which we apply them, so that justice, equanimity, and liberty, might prevail, in order to continue to "secure the blessings of liberty to ourselves and our posterity."

James Madison, American Founder, puts it this way, in Publius / Federalist Papers No. 51:

"And happily for *the republican cause,* the practicable sphere may be carried to a very great extent by a judicious modification and mixture of *the federal principle.*"

Things would continue to go well as long as we persevere in subscribing to the substantive rights and due process rights that formulate our

IT'S A CONTINUUM

adherence to constitutional principles of a *republican Form of government* that preserves the spirit of accommodation in agreeing that the general government will respect and protect the prerogatives of citizens to have regional autonomy and local self-government.

"The United States shall guarantee to every State in this Union a republican form of government, and shall protect each of them against invasion; and on application of the legislature, or of the executive (when the legislature cannot be convened) against domestic violence." (Constitution of the United States of America, Article IV, Section 4).

Division of powers, Separation of powers, Checks-and-Balances, local self-determination, official self-restraint and self-control, and protection of free institutions that reflect the intimate interests of We the People in ways-and-means, mechanisms and processes, that operate, consistently with integrity, dispatch, and alacrity, to defend and preserve both prerequisites and necessities that qualify our Form of free government, with the characteristics of a *representative democracy*.

In Publius / Federalist Papers No. 48, James Madison, American Founder, elucidates this matter by stating:

"An *elective despotism* is not the government we fought for; but one which should not only be founded on free principles, but in which the powers of government should be so divided and balanced among several bodies of magistracy as that no one could transcend their legal limits without being effectually checked and restrained by the others. For this reason that convention which passed the ordinance of government laid its foundation on this basis, that the legislative, executive and judiciary departments should be separate and distinct, so that no person should exercise the powers of more than one of them at the same time."

Thus, dear friends: Liberty is real! Freedom is real! Let us study, learn, and know how to help them flourish in accordance with the loving kindness of our mighty Creator who authored all our inalienable constitutional "Bill of Rights."

We fervently hope, in righteous faith, because Christ Jesus is the "author and finisher of our faith." Christ will "perfect" our faith so that we become "as perfect as our heavenly Father is perfect."

For perfect love takes away fear by faith in the loving kindness of God through Christ's sacrificial death on the Cross by whose precious blood our transgressions and iniquities are blotted out. Thus, We can spiritually aspire to have "perfect understanding" so that in applying the principles of Free government, our errors can be minimized but also fastidiously corrected with the least amount of effort, because we are diligent in maintaining fidelity to their substance and foundation as laid in Christ, not only in faith, but also in word, letter, spirit, truth and deed. (Matthew 5:43–48; 1 Corinthians 3:10–23; 13:8–13; Hebrews 12:1–2; 1 John 4:13–21).

Only Christ can "progressively perfect" our works and deeds, even as we are diligently and earnestly co-laboring together, so as to approach and come closer and closer to "a more perfect Union," as long as we shall always remain: "One nation, UNDER GOD, indivisible, with liberty and justice for ALL."

That we don't remain as we are without ever "continually renewing ourselves," but are always improving and ameliorating our system of free government, "from one degree of perfection to another," towards the fullest fulfillment of our well-being and most complete satisfaction of our general welfare. (Romans 12:1–2; 2 Corinthians 3:12–18; Hebrews 11:39; 12:1–11).

We cannot "stand still:" yet, we "must also move ahead," albeit, cautiously and prudently, justly and peacefully, compassionately and lawfully, freely and openly, deliberately and diligently, in order, not only to preserve the Good we have attained thus far, but to also redress the wrongs that have been "afflicting our Union" since its very Founding in the year of our Lord One thousand Seven Hundred and Seventy-six.

How do we do that? Why do we speak of America's Founders, even in the light of their shortcomings and in spite of their numerous failures? Because We The People can hold on to the good foundation they've laid out for us to follow, as Christ remains our guiding light, precious Hope, and elective predestination. (Romans 8:26–30; 1 Peter 2:1–16; 2 Peter 1:3–11).

God-given Liberty had to "begin somewhere!" And that was in 1776 AD! Thus, as of 2018, it's been over Two Hundred and Forty-Two years ago! For God works His miracles also, and especially, also, through We the People! For, by "all standards of the Human Condition" that "our sinful Human Nature" might engender or engineer and by which "biological Entropy" of our flesh can be measured: "America is A Miracle!"

Well, General George Washington at the end of the Revolutionary War against the British Empire in 1783 AD, did not declare himself "emperor" or "king" to then let Americans know "what rights they had."

General Washington took-off his military uniform, returned his officer commission to the Continental Congress, and went back to his farm to plant and harvest his crops.

IT'S A CONTINUUM

General Washington set the tone for our republic as a free constitutional representative form of democratic government, once and for all.

By dissociating ourselves from the irrational carnal passions emerging from the Human heart, e.g., lust for unjust and corrupt power, "lust of the flesh, lust of the eyes, and the pride of life" (1 John 2:15–17), we can then dedicate ourselves to nourishing the "spiritual anchors" given to us by Christ Jesus for our souls, sums of which, will progressively establish "a path to improvement" and "a course to amelioration," from our earnest colabors and works within the fervent and rich wellsprings of our righteous faith in God. (Romans 1:16–23; 6:12–14; 1 John 2:28–29).

The fleshly body must eventually die, regardless of how it looks externally, regardless of how numerous its material possessions! We reach old age to have our skin wrinkled and dry, our libido abated, our energies failing, and our health declining.

But we have a great and mighty Hope: For in God's Word, through Samuel the priest, (1 Samuel 16:6–7) we learn that: God judges according to the heart, not like mortals who judge according to mere outward external appearance, e.g., not according to race, ethnicity, birthplace, skin color, height, flesh, or weight! All individual Persons must eventually die, regardless of race or ethnicity, place of birth, amount of wealth or material possessions! Death comes regardless of how wealthy or what amounts of material possessions we own; what kind of job one does; if we have "riches untold," such as stock-and-bonds portfolios, and certificates of deposit, and financial securities, etc. . ... Still, death does come!

But also Life eternal comes thereafter! For we are not without Hope. We have "Christ in us, the Hope of Glory." (Colossians 1:27–29; Hebrews 11:1–2).

Jesus proclaimed to us in John 6:63: "The words I have spoken to you are spirit and life. Life is in the spirit; the flesh is of no avail!"

And, again, in Scriptures, (2 Corinthians 3:17–18), we learn that "God is Spirit and where the Spirit of the Lord is, there is liberty." And our Liberty is given to us by God, to be free in Christ Jesus, and not to submit again to another yoke of bondage; but to do all things in honor of Jesus Christ whose precious love we embody and "carry with us" wherever we go! (Galatians 5:1; 13–18).

And that God looks for those who worship Him "in spirit and in truth." (John 4:23–26). Thus, Liberty is not random acts of thoughtless anarchy but a self-conscious decision to willfully and deliberately do what is right in the sight of God in the face of Christ who gave us His peace and His love that will never leave or forsake us: "Lo, I am with you always, even to the end of the world!" (Matthew 28:18–20).

God gave us liberty in order to free us from bondage to sin, wickedness, and evil, so that, we can "truly be ourselves" as "children of God," who are "born of the spirit," to think and to act "unto the image and likeness of God," while we are diligently "trained in righteousness," through a deeper understanding of biblical principles that, as "self-evident Realities," affirm, nourish, practice, nurture and preserve: love, peace, liberty, justice, freedom, and prosperity, sums of which, impelling us "from within," to commit ourselves to repent of our sins in order to obtain forgiveness, by observing and following God's Word of Truth in Christ Jesus who has given us "new life" by the "rebirth of our spirit." Thus, by that, "we walk by faith, not by sight." (Romans 10:14–17; 1 Corinthians 13:8–13; 14:33; 15:33; 2 Corinthians 5:4–9; 2 Timothy 2:21–26; 3:16–17).

Loving and clinging to material-physical things, i.e., "the love of money," or the love of "the mammon of unrighteousness," "is the root of all sorts of evil." "To love and cling to these perishable things" that we leave behind when we pass away, is a detriment, a disparagement, and disservice to our earthly living "as righteous and saved Spirit-Beings." (Matthew 6:24; 1 Timothy 6:9–10).

It's alright to be rich and wealthy, "by the sweat of one's brow" (Genesis 3: 19), as God in His loving kindness allows us to have socio-political economic systems within which are embedded the laws and regulations securing and protecting our "rights to private property." (Luke 12:4–7; 16–21).

But God's Word in Christ Jesus exhorts us to first seek His kingdom and His righteousness, and then, all these things "shall be added" unto us. We lose nothing but gain "a whole Universe!" (Psalms 24:1; Isaiah 66:1; Matthew 6:33; 19:23–26; Luke 12:15).

Loving God in service to our fellow Human Beings, in service to one another, must be prioritized in ways that magnify "the better angels of our nature." (President Abraham Lincoln, First Inaugural Address, March 4, 1861).

Serving God by "doing the truth in love" (Ephesians 4:15), puts "our hearts in the right place." When every person desires to serve every other person with good thinking from godly faith that yields good deeds, then, are not our needs indeed taken care of? Don't we truly become "our brother's keepers;" or rather, "one another's keepers!" Still, we carry our own loads

IT'S A CONTINUUM

or burdens in accordance with our capabilities as well as bear each other's loads and burdens by the grace of God who entreats us unto righteousness (Galatians 6:2). For "love covers a multitude of sins;" love always finds the right way to do something good! (1 Corinthians 13:1-13; James 5:19-20).

Where love, charity, generosity, hospitality, hard work, prosperity, compassion, and thanksgiving govern the utilization of exceeding outpourings from our prosperous abundance that's flooding our Human society, there is no lack, want, or need; for all are properly fulfilled. (2 Corinthians 8:8-15).

Even though, in terms of material-physical possessions — which we all will leave behind anyway when we do pass away as "there is no U-haul behind a hearse" — there might not yet be "wealth equality," in the sense of equally distributed ownership of property holdings, goods, products, and services and allocations of natural and social resources, but, one thing that we do know: No one will starve, no one will be homeless, no one will be illiterate, all will have proper medical care, etc. . . Not one of us will suffer lack or loss! For there is indeed "plenty to go around!" We have a whole Planet and a whole Universe where God has implanted and embedded every resource necessary to fulfill all our needs, both spiritual and physical! The problem then is not "in the hardware," but rather "in the software!" But as "the hardware" can be "modified" in service to our real needs, e.g., in cold seasons we have in-house heat from electric or gas furnaces; so too, can "the software" be "perfected" in the love of Christ and the peace of His Spirit, i.e., Jesus is our original foundation and substance, for "all the moral-spiritual food" that we have ever needed! Spiritually speaking, Jesus is "the bread of life!" (John 6:32-40; 44-51).

For "material and social equality" will "naturally flow" from our transcendent godly understanding and knowledge of "our common spiritual equality" as "children of God" who are "born of the Spirit" through the regeneration of our hearts and the transformation of our minds for "newness of life" on the Earth. (Romans 12:1-2).

We know that "we're only passing through!" But why should it be "a hell on Earth" instead of "a paradise regained?"

Hence why our Lord Jesus told us that: "The kingdom of God is within you!" (Mark 10:25-27; 12:29-31; Luke 6:20-31; 6:35-36; 17:20-21). "All the good that is ours in Christ Jesus" will just overflow unto one another's lives to fulfill every innate Human need with which God endowed us from natural conception to natural death. (Psalms 24:1; Philemon 6). For God is

Spirit and He attends to all our innate Human needs as Spirit-Beings who are being molded and formed unto, not only His own image and likeness, but also, by faith, unto Christ-likeness for mature workmanship in the perfection of our souls! (Ephesians 2:8-10; Hebrews 12:1-2).

Are not Human Beings like us mortals, from the diaper to the coffin, "in charge of everything" that happens to one another in our society? God does "work in mysterious ways," even "through other people!" Do unto others as you would have them do unto you! This commandment has been with us from the very beginning, nay, even before the foundation of the world! (Psalms 146:9; Jeremiah 49:11; Matthew 5:13-16; 43-48; 25:31-46; James 1:27).

From production to consumption, from scarcity to abundance, from slavery to freedom, from bondage to liberty, and from misery to joy, etc. …, Human Beings influence and impact each other's earthly destiny, and even each other's eternal destiny!

Hence, reasons why focusing on mortal flesh-and-blood such as "the obsession with genealogy" that emphasizes "genetic lineage," wars against "worshipping God in spirit and in truth."

Christ Jesus rose from the dead; God is Spirit! Why are we commanded "to not worship the flesh?" We are all waiting for the eventual coffin while, in the mean time, having to "relieve" ourselves daily of "entropic waste" generated throughout our way of life. None is good but God; the flesh is to no avail. Our righteousness is "as filthy rags." So, let's stop focusing such massive amounts of energy and emotional investment in such a thing as mortal flesh! (Isaiah 64:6; Mark 10: 18; John 6:63). We are commanded to love God in spirit and in truth and to do the truth in love towards one another! Spirit matters! Flesh dies, putrefies, degrades, and becomes only dust! Our value and worth as Human Beings stem only from our having been created by God unto becoming like His resurrected Son, Jesus Christ, also! To become as sons and daughters of God living in a material Universe from which we obtain "all the good that is ours in Christ Jesus!"

For God had said "Let there be light; and there was light and God saw that the light was good!" The things that are, come from the things that are not visible: Did not our abstract invisible Minds invent, design, create, and manufacture the electronic Computers that today serve our administrative and functional needs? Where was the Computer before then? Christ told us, "the kingdom of God is within you!" (Luke 17:20-21). Thus, spirit creates but flesh only consumes! But, at the same time, God has empowered

IT'S A CONTINUUM

us through the love and peace of Christ, so that we can create that which is only good, not only for the preservation, general welfare, and protection of our Biological Organisms, but also for the spiritual well-being of our living Souls, as "purveyors of created things" in our society that the flesh needs to consume or utilize "for life and godliness." (2 Timothy 3:14–17).

Thus, "ancestral worship" or an obsession with "genealogical lineage" that displaces our innate need to worship and glorify God, in spirit and in truth, is the nemesis of our reaching a beneficent, richer, and deeper understanding of our "common spiritual equality."

The Holy Bible in Christ Jesus "spiritualizes" Humanity; but "genealogy" for its own sake only degrades us to mere carnal flesh or to mere pieces of meat having only a physical-biological history in this vast barren Universe as opposed to owning a heavenly beginning predestined for spiritual perfection unto mature Humanness!

Satan focuses on the physical, on the material; in short, "on appearance of the flesh!" But Flesh is still sinful and mortal! Flesh is living at the same time that it carries the Entropy of ultimate death within its very genes!

Life, more abundant, as well as eternal Life, is in the Spirit of God in Christ Jesus who rose from the dead to defeat the deceitful wicked evil underhanded machinations of the Devil!

For, "ancestral lineage" is the history of "death of Humanity" from ancestor to ancestor that the flesh carries in its very genes!

Let us prosper as we reproduce Life and the history of the living rather than the worship of dead biological ancestors whose sins and crimes are ever before us, from ownership of slaves to perpetrating genocide: From Pharaoh to Caesar; from Alexander (misnamed) the Great to Napoleon Bonaparte; from Hitler and Mussolini to Lenin and Stalin, etc. . . There is nothing good in fleshly genealogy, which can only instill a sort of "false pride" in things that are dead, from the beginning to end, without any hope of ever being revived! Who wants to bring back slavery or ownership of Human Beings by other Human Beings? Resurrection of the dead, — with a "new spiritual body:" for what is physical is physical and what is spiritual is spiritual — comes only through Christ Jesus who commands us to worship God in spirit and in truth as we love one another in accordance with His grace and mercy!

"Biological genealogical worship" of dead ancestors "ending only in a box interred 6-feet under," diverts attention, desire, intent, will, and interest from the more transcendent abstract, spiritual-moral character of Human

Beings, who are "created unto the image and likeness of God;" as well as stultifies our creative qualities, emotional intelligence, and intellectual attributes that "make us who we really are," as Human Beings, as "Spirit-Beings" who have "the Mind of Christ!" (1 Corinthians 2:14–16).

For we are "not in the dark," no; we are no longer ignorant of the Truth that sets us all free: We who've known "the life and times" of our Lord and Savior Jesus Christ on the Earth as well as the life to come because of His resurrection from the dead and His promise to return!

So much energy, resources, and time are wasted on focusing on "dead flesh" that our children are almost compelled to worship, even dinosaur bones, in museums where past or extinct Species of animals are being kept — Dinosaurs are dead animals!

Please, "let's get a life in Christ Jesus!" We are called by God to be "our brother's keepers" and not the "keeper of dead dinosaurs' bones!"

God is Spirit and we worship Him "in spirit and in truth." Jesus came as a man; but He rose from the dead as God! (2 Corinthians 5:14–21). Therefore, Jesus is no longer "just a Man;" but He ascended unto Heaven: He is Spirit; and His Holy Spirit indwells us! Let us be reconciled with God in Christ our Savior!

So, why do we unearth dinosaur bones which we display in museums for almost "worship-viewing?"

And in the same manner, even if we can go as far back in the past, down to the 1600's, if possible, in order to find out about our "dead biological ancestors" that delineate our "family tree," when we do, what heavenly purpose or spiritual end does that fulfill? — which happens very rarely to "go that far back into the past," especially, when record-keeping was sparsely maintained, or rarely practiced for Human history or posterity, not only due to the ubiquity of illiteracy amongst the masses of people who were then, mere "subjects of His majesty the king," or mere "serfs" in bondsman-service to "the manorial lord;" but also due to various deadly wars of conquests and mayhem that might have destroyed, even the sparsely kept records existing then, such as "the burning of Alexandria" and "the burning of Rome!"

Our dead biological ancestors were not living "in the good old days," folks! As the philosopher Thomas Hobbs puts it: "Life was nasty, brutish, and short!"

But thanks be to God our Father in Heaven for His indescribable gift: Christ Jesus by whose Spirit we are renewed daily into conformation to

IT'S A CONTINUUM

God's character-qualities in us! (2 Corinthians 3:12–18; 4:1–7). It is not only "cleanliness that's next to godliness," but rather Love and Peace, Truth and Liberty, Justice and Prosperity amongst us, that are "next to godliness!" We have no excuse! No, not any longer! For "the kingdom of God is within us!"

And then, once we obtain information on our "biological lineage," what do we do with it? What purpose does it serve now that we have such "genealogical lineage information?" To have false pride in ourselves for knowing the sins and crimes of our biological ancestors? We think not! Remember the "Salem Witch Trials?" Remember "the Spanish Inquisition?" Remember enslavement of Black people? Remember that our "biological ancestors" did "not see fit," to allow, even white American women to vote in their representative elections, in "our representative elections?" What is it exactly to be "proud of?" Except that we can thank God for their spiritual accomplishments in establishing our system of free government so that we can, not only preserve the Good they accomplished by the Grace and Mercy of our Creator, but also, so that we can endeavor earnestly, and without dissimulation, to redress the wrongs which we know had been perpetrated in times past against people in our midst whom we are entreated and commanded to love, as "kindred spirit-beings," born of God, born anew in the Spirit, in Christ Jesus, our compassionate Lord and Savior!

"Our biological ancestors" or "genealogical lineage" died, like we also, will eventually, ultimately, die! Only bones remain! The flesh returns to dust! God is the God of the living and not of the dead!

But we are "citizens of Heaven" only "passing through" mortal existence; and as spirit-beings, we return to our original Form! What is physical is physical in the likeness of Adam and Eve; but what is spiritual is spiritual in the living likeness of Christ Jesus who is crowned in glory for our sakes, for our benefit, for our good, for our well-being, for our general welfare: For God shows no partiality! For God shows no favoritism! God is not a man that he should lie or take a bribe!

We're all "created equal" from the womb to the tomb! But death is "swallowed up in victory!" We inherit eternal life in the kingdom of God, in "the world to come!" (John 14:6–7; Romans 2:1–11; 1 Corinthians 5:51–58; Galatians 4:19; Colossians 2:17–18; 3:15–17; 1 Timothy 5:21).

As mortality overtook "our biological ancestors," which evolutionists hold "descended from apes," in the same way, death will eventually overtake us.

This kind of death, biological, happens to us all! But the life that is already in us in the Spirit of God through our risen Savior, Christ Jesus, prevails; and not the mortal flesh that "ends up in a box 6-feet under!"

It is not the fact of being interested in "knowing one's family tree" that is a "carnal problem;" for it is normal to appreciate one's immediate family or distant relatives in a way that transcends simple friendship and neighborliness. Our memories of them are precious to us! But not before God! Not to replace God! God forbid we should worship our dead ancestors rather than invest our inner-soul energies in worshipping the true God of love, the true God of peace, the true God of righteousness, and the true God of eternal life! (John 3:3; 3:16: 17:3).

God must have transcendent priority in our lives, created and formed, for faithful spiritual worship and for doing good deeds! (1 Corinthians 8:5–6; 15:31–35; 2 Corinthians 5:10; 7:1).

But rather, when it becomes idolatry, or is worshipped in the place of God, such that, "ancestral worship" diverts our activities, attention, desires, and interests from true authentic genuine worship that belongs: Only to Almighty God, our sovereign and only Creator, our heavenly Father; then, God is no longer the supreme priority in our lives through Christ's Holy Spirit! And that is to our disadvantage, and even, to our death! For we are entreated and commanded to love our neighbor as our own selves! (Matthew 4:17; 5:1–16; 43–48; 6:9–13 KJV; 6:33; John 6:63; Romans 1:16–23; Galatians 4:3,9; Colossians 2:8, 20).

When we pray, we pray for God's Will to be "done on Earth as it is in Heaven!" We go to the Father but through the living Christ who rose from the dead, not through deceased ancestors! "God is God of the living and not of the dead!" They could not "save themselves!" They surely cannot "save us!" Our ancestors are "dead and gone!" Only their bones remain! (Matthew 22:32; Marc 2:25–28).

"Pentecost" — the indwelling of God's Holy Spirit in Christ Jesus — Yes, "Pentecost" happens only with the living and not the dead! God is the God of the living and not of the dead! (Matthew 22:32; John 14:6–7; Acts 2:1–42; 4:12).

The Word of God in the Holy Bible calls us to spiritual worship of God and not to genealogical worship of our dead biological ancestors:

"Abraham believed God and it was reckoned to him as righteousness." His faith was righteous and not his mortal body, not his mortal flesh!

IT'S A CONTINUUM

We thus are "the Seed of Abraham" by our faith and not by our "genealogical biological connection" to him as a mortal man, as a dead ancestor!

God cares primarily about our faith in Him through the Holy Spirit of His living resurrected Son, Jesus Christ, our "King of kings and Lord of lords." (Genesis 15:6; Romans 4:3; Hebrews 11:1-3; 11:6; Revelation 19:11-16).

It is Abraham's faith in God that "set him apart," "separated him" and "consecrated him" to God, from other people, and not his biological lineage or ethnic heritage. He was from Ur, of the Chaldees, — In the flesh, Abram (later called Abraham or "father of many nations) — was a "Chaldean" from ancient Sumer in Babylon! Hence, why those who are the called according to God's purpose are called in His Name after Isaac, the Seed of Abraham's faith, — (SEED, as from Genesis 3:15 in fulfillment of God's living word of truth in Christ Jesus; and not "offspring" or "descendant," as some other bible translations might say, in order to reduce Jesus' immaculate Holy Spirit conception to only "biological lineage" to suit "fleshly interests," like "the Pharisees and the doctors of the law who rejected the purposes of God for themselves!" For they had transmogrified the temple "from a house of prayer" unto "a den of thieves!" (Luke 7:24:30; 19:41-48; Romans 3:9-18; 4:10-13; 8:26-31 KJV).

Abraham's SEED, "the SEED of Woman," is Jesus Christ in whom we live, made manifest on the Earth and in Heaven, as the resurrected Son of God. (Acts 3:19-26; Romans 4:1-25; 7:6; 8:28; Galatians 3:23-29 KJV; Galatians 4:21-28 KJV).

Why are some trying to rebuild what God Himself has declared obsolete? (Galatians 2:18-20; Hebrews 8:13; 13:8).

God has done "a new thing!" (Isaiah 42:6-9; 43:18; 48:6; 62:2; 65:17; 66:22). Jesus said through the Prophet Isaiah, "Behold, I make all things new!" Faith as small as a mustard seed can even "move mountains." God's people, "the Israel of God," are called "by a new name:" Christians! (Psalms 98:1; Jeremiah 31:31-33; Matthew 9:16-17; 62; 13:51-52; 17:20-21; Luke 11:9-10; John 4:24-26; 6:40; 46-48; 9:39-41; Acts 5:20; 11:23-26.)

Isaac was "as good as dead," except that the angel of God stopped Abraham from sacrificing him on the fiery altar erected for that purpose.

"By faith Abraham, when he was tested, offered up Isaac, and he who had received the promises was ready to offer up his only son, of whom it was said, 'Through Isaac shall your Seed be named. KJV' " (Genesis 21:12; Hebrews 11:18).

WHY ONLY JESUS!

(Abram was from Ur of the Chaldees in ancient Babylon and all flesh descendants or biological offspring of Abraham died as mortal Humans: from Ishmael to Jacob, they did die, as every other mortal Human Being.) Thus, we are NOT called by God "in pursuit of fleshly genealogy," but we are called after "the Seed of Abraham's Faith in God," to belong to His Heavenly Family through our resurrected brother, Jesus Christ, whose Holy Spirit lives within us, who, in the likeness of "the saved Isaac;" Jesus, "the first born of the dead," was also offered as a living sacrifice on the Cross as an atonement for our sins! Isaac who was "as good as dead," was not sacrificed on the altar because God had "saved" him from Abram's knife; but Jesus did die on the Cross, to rise from the dead, as the Son of the Living God! So, Jesus was God from the womb to the tomb — He was conceived by God's Holy Spirit in the womb of the Virgin Mary ("a biological womb!") and rose from the dead after being entombed within the bowels of the Earth ("an earthly womb!") hewn from the dust of the ground of the Earth! But Jesus "did not return to dust" as mortal men do; for as "the SEED of Woman," He rose from the dead as "the SEED of Abram's Faith," in the likeness of Isaac. Hence, those who are called by God's Name enter into God's Kingdom through the Seed of Isaac, the seed of faith, and not through the biological lineage of Abram, nor Ishmael, nor Jacob whose name God had changed to "Israel" in order to bring Messiah Christ Jesus through a "saved Remnant" of the "children of Jacob in-the-flesh" or "the children of Israel in-the-flesh!" Which was a shadow of things to come, "the Israel of God," the Church, "the Body of Christ," the substance or foundation that was to come, as promised, as prophesied, which is only Christ Jesus! Remember:

"The Pharisees and the doctors of the law rejected the purposes of God for themselves." Therefore: "The stone that the builders rejected has become the chief cornerstone! And the Lord has done this and it is marvelous in our eyes. This is the day that the Lord has made, let us rejoice and be glad in it!" (Psalms 89:46–48; 118:19–25; John 1:1–18; Matthew 21:42; Mark 12:10; Luke 20:17; 1 Corinthians 8:1–6; Galatians 6:6–18).

We, Christians, as Human Beings "born anew in the spirit" through the Holy Spirit of our risen Savior Christ Jesus, are sealed as the true heirs of God's kingdom. Because, as we are "named through Isaac" who "represented in a figure," who "symbolized," or who "foreshadowed" God's love for us in sending Jesus Christ, His only begotten Son, as a sacrificial atonement, as a fit-and-proper holy and righteous propitiation for our sins: We, believers with faith in Christ Jesus are "the Israel of God," and therefore, are

IT'S A CONTINUUM

the genuine spiritual Seed of Faith (From Genesis 3:15); we are the authentic genuine "faith-Seed of Abraham" whose "seed of faith" was "reckoned to him as righteousness" while he yet lived! "God is the God of the living and not of the dead!" (Genesis 15:6; Romans 4:3; Galatians 6:13-18; Philippians 3:1-3).

We, Christians, are the true heirs of Abraham, "father of FAITH," for we have faith in Christ as Abraham believed God in faith, which was credited to him as "righteousness."

We Christians are "the Israel of God," because the Scriptures are fulfilled in Christ who lives in us who are "circumcised of heart," and not of the flesh. For if removing a piece of flesh, the foreskin from a part of the body, brought "salvation," then, all amputees might have inherited God's kingdom! But we are the "true circumcision" who have given up "the heart of stone," and "the temple of stone," (Psalms 24:1; Isaiah 66:1), to be transformed into "tablets of human heart" upon which the love of God in Christ Jesus is fully written: Which is the only "God-approved value" or "God-called worth" to ever be put on mortal flesh! (Jeremiah 31:33; Romans 2:27-29; 2 Corinthians 3:1-3; Philippians 3:1-11).

The "syndrome of genealogical obsession," e.g., "ancestral worship," partakes of the same psychological-emotional underpinnings that direct our "fleshly desires to hoard" material-physical things worshipped as "property" or "possessions," due to "the love of money," on the one hand. But, on the other hand, we brought nothing into this world and we leave it with nothing as well. Only bones remain — no longer belonging to us, but to "the dust of the ground of the earth" to which God had said we'd return! (Genesis 3:19; 1 Timothy 6:6-10).

However, due to Human Beings attempting to "find an identity" or "to feel valuable" in the material things that we possess and own, — subconsciously, That, in accordance with "habeas corpus," we have a physical biological body needing physical things to live, such as foodstuff made-up of plants and animal meats, etc... — that "worthless misidentification" causes us to lose experiencing "the joy of the spirit," by not immersing ourselves in partaking of God's saving power that enlightens our lives. (Philippians 4:4-13).

It is often asked: "What would Jesus do?" Well, when we're filled with the Spirit, God's charcter-qualities then overflow as an outpouring of love and charity towards our fellow Human Beings, in compassionate ways that mirror and reflect "God's image and likeness" within our hearts, within us.

The will-power of love of Christ Jesus, risen from the dead, who ascended unto Heaven, sent us the Comforter, God's very own Holy Spirit, as promised, as prophesied! (2 Corinthians 12:19; Ephesians 4:14–16; 2 Corinthians 8:15.)

But the Truth hurts our ego sometimes, especially when it appears to carry a tone of condemnation or seems to embrace a resonance of blame at which we take offence rather than "deal with the truth" in an honest way, due to our bias, favoritism towards a tribe or clan, partisanship in a certain cause, partiality to selfish worldly ambitions, foolhardy arrogance, or plain prideful vainglory. Scriptures proclaim: "But God exalts the humble and opposes the proud!" (James 4:4–8; 2 Peter 5:5–11).

When viewed from the vantage point of suffering from "worldly grief," shame and guilt follow, accompanied by resentment and revenge. But when we have experienced "godly grief" that brings true repentance and leads to salvation, then we do well in "grieving over our sins." For, by that character-quality imparted to us by our Creator, God's will for us, results, in that, we are saved, redeemed, and sanctified! Thus, "doing the Truth in love," means exactly that: That the Church be "the pillar and bulwark of the Truth." (1 Corinthians 1:26–31; 3:9; 2 Corinthians 7:10–11; 1 Timothy 3:14–16).

In that vein, the Apostle Peter, proclaiming the Word of God, says of faithless idolaters: "They promise them freedom while they themselves are slaves of corruption; for whatever overcomes a man, to that he is enslaved." (2 Peter 2:19)

And as Peter, the Apostle of Christ, continues: "It has happened to them according to the true proverb, The dog turns back to its own vomit, and the sow is washed to wallow again in the mire." (2 Peter 2:22).

Please, don't misunderstand! As intimated above: We can't help desiring "to own things!" Our physical body needs physical biological things! Thus, "private property" is as inevitable as "genealogical lineage" is undeniably a fact of Human existence on the Earth. For due to the First Law of Bio-genesis, it is Human Beings who "biologically reproduce" or "give birth" to other Human beings — thus, only we can wear the shirts on our backs belonging to our own bodies! Each one of us wears his or her own shoes on his or her own two feet.

But remember always: We are first and foremost: Spirit-Beings! Thus, reasons why, Jesus, "the bread of eternal life," told us that "Man does not live by bread alone but by every word that proceeds out of the mouth of God." (Matthew 4:1–11).

IT'S A CONTINUUM

"Spiritual rebirth" for mind transformation unto love, peace, righteousness, humility, justice, and compassion happens only through our Lord and Savior Jesus Christ in whom we are "born anew," "born of the Spirit," "born of God." (John 1:1–18).

But through "ancestral biological lineage," from Adam and Eve, through Cain and Abel, Jacob and Esau, onwards, the Holy Bible, plainly tells us that we have inherited Sinfulness as much as our physical-material environment is plagued by Entropy.

"The dust of the ground of the Earth" from whence God had created us, as "biological flesh," was also "cursed" due to disobedience by Adam and Eve of God's commandments in the Garden of Eden. And Cain murdered his own brother, Abel! There is nothing good in biological flesh! No one is good but God! (Luke 18:19)

And Jesus said that while he was in the world as a Man, as one of us, as Son of Man, walking on the Earth in biological flesh: The flesh is of no account, of no avail, and "counts for nothing." (John 6:63). Hence, why God raised Him from the dead so that we might inherit the Seal of God's Spirit within our very Souls, entreating us to glorify God in the Universe by our faith and by our works! (2 Corinthians 1:1–24; Ephesians 1:1–14; 4:29–32).

Hence, why "We walk by faith, not by sight!" Only through God had Jesus the eternal power to raise Lazarus from the dead, in the likeness of Isaac. Jesus also rose from the dead after He was entombed following His crucifixion. (John 11:41–44; 2 Corinthians 5:7; Hebrews 11:1–3; 17–19).

In addition, having those things that are necessary for fulfillment of our real needs, such as for food, clothing, shelter, water, sanitation, medical care, and education — We can't help it! The need to pursue fulfillment of these natural necessities is seeded, rooted, and imprinted in our very DNA.

Jesus told us that God knows we need such things (Mattew 6:33). Hence, God's establishment of society with agreed upon laws and rules that regulate our Economic System so that there are right ways, resources, avenues, channels, and means, instituted for fulfilling those necessary needs.

But, our bodies, which are physical-biological, breathing Oxygen from earth atmosphere, also crave to possess, hold, keep, hoard, and own "things material," such as stocks, bonds, gold, and silver, cars, boats, planes, houses, and even "biological ancestors," from all of which, we obtain "a false sense of pride, arrogance, and vanity," because we also have desires rooted in "the love of Money," due to our succumbing to temptations attached to "the lusts of the eyes, the lusts of the flesh and the pride of life."

So pervasive is the "acquisitive instinct," that our thinking processes, e.g., "consumerism," can often be overtaken by the tendency to "hoard physical material things" that appear to give us "a false sense of power, security, and control" over other people and over things in society — it is a "false sense of security, power and control" because wealth and riches, i.e., excessive lavish possession of physical-material things, cannot give us neither perfection nor immortality in biological flesh! We still die eventually as "flawed Mortals!"

But God by His grace and Mercy, and loving kindness allows us to make use of such things while we are temporarily living on the Earth. (Luke 12:19–21).

Thus, if not checked-and-balanced by "a spirit of power, love, and sound mind," (2 Timothy 1:6–7) our "acquisitive instincts" can become very destructive, e.g., wars are fought for "conquering territory," "making slaves" of other Human Beings, or amassing spoils as "loot and booty."

Hence, why Scriptures tell us, that the flesh is always warring against the spirit, hence, why the kingdom of God continues "to suffer violence" and "violent men take it by force." (Psalms 24:1; Matthew 11:12; Romans 8:6–9; 2 Corinthians 10:26).

That form of ingrained violence, turning now against the Self, also overspills unto other aspects of our lives when we fail to seek the presence of God in Christ's Holy Spirit to help us overcome such temptations as to "bail out."

Isn't the rate of suicide amongst our young people, children, and middle-aged citizens climbing to alarming levels, especially through "opiate addiction," and/or abuse of other illicit drugs that alter thought processes and sabotage emotional awareness, to the point of becoming not only lethal to self, but also, at times, fatal to others?

"The monkey with the most toys" ends up losing everything! There is something very disturbing, if not wrong, with "hoarding material things" that we can utilize "only one at a time," and with which, we'll eventually part, when we die, — "no U-haul behind a hearse" — while other Human Beings are starving to death, lack medical health care, are plagued by illiteracy, or are in bondage to common illnesses and diseases that technological inventions, such as, discoveries of penicillin and vaccinations have already abated.

Such "medical technologies" reign supreme, amongst certain people-groups, in certain regions of the Earth while in other areas of the globe, other people-groups are suffering daily from illnesses and diseases, "long-conquered by those medical technologies."

But when love and charity govern utilization of resources, voluminous outpourings of prosperous abundance earned through hard work and honest labor, ought to be acquired, in kind, in accordance with laws that ensure that there is no lack for anyone in our society. (2 Corinthians 8:12–15).

Satan fell from God's grace! (Isaiah 14:12–20; 28:14–19; Ezekiel 28:1–19; Luke 10:17–20).

The devil was cast out of Heaven by our Creator who then gave us Life, "life more abundant," and eternal life; so that as His children, in faithful communion with His Holy Spirit, we might become, through Christ Jesus, fellow-heirs of His kingdom.

✷✷✷

THE MEANING OF PURPOSIVE HUMAN LIVING

We've discovered that our reliance solely upon mere material-physical possessions in order to "gain an identity," from which to obtain a false sense of self-esteem, in order to feel worthy and valuable, develop a self-concept, or gain a sense of purpose for existence, becomes an exercise in futility, vainglory, foolhardiness, and vanity.

Only in accepting and receiving the sacrificial propitiation of our sins by Christ on the Cross can we really understand and know our true selves, gain our true identity as children of God whose tribulations, troubles, and problems, and dilemmas can be "put at the foot of the Cross" as we "unload our burdens upon Christ's shoulders" where there is comfort, meaning, purpose, life, and Truth for Living the right way on the Earth; so that hopelessness and desperation will not take root in our souls to impel us from within to commit acts of destruction against our own selves and others, such as, in suicide or murder. (Isaiah 9:6–7).

Hence, why God wants us to firmly and fervently rely and depend on Him through the Holy Spirit of Christ Jesus, His resurrected Son, our Savior and Lord: "I can do all things through Christ who gives me strength." (Philippians 4:4–13).

Our temporary lives do matter because life is a blessing, a gift from our loving Creator by whose Holy Spirit we can commune with our Savior Jesus Christ.

In addition, we do not die as soon as we're born, but grow, develop, mature and age, as we endeavor to peaceably, justly, and lawfully prosper for ourselves and our posterity, as we also contribute to our neighborhoods and to our society.

IT'S A CONTINUUM

But let us remember to love God and our fellow Human Beings, first, as we continue to pray for God's Will to be "done on Earth as it is in Heaven." For no matter what we achieve in this world while temporarily living in biological flesh, we still eventually, inescapably, and unavoidably must admit to its brevity when compared to Eternity.

God, our Creator, has no beginning and no end because He is eternal, Omniscient, Omnipotent, Ever-present or Immanent, and Sovereign. But, we, on the other hand, are "only passing through." God knows that and that's why He has compassion for us. For by His grace and Mercy, He sent Jesus Christ, His only begotten Son, our resurrected heavenly brother, to save us from all this Sinfulness and Entropy that are assailing our "best intentions" and "our best desires" to live righteously and faithfully on the Earth until Christ returns! (2 Peter 3:1–18).

And that's why we can't just lay down and die! God forbid! "Away from me Satan, for it is written, Thou shalt only worship the Lord thy God and only Him shalt thou serve." (Matthew 4:10).

Therefore, we still go through all the steps and stages of growth and development, in our lives, that Human Beings experience from infancy to adulthood: From obtaining an education to getting employed, from planning for the future and realizing one's goals in life, to God-ordained marriage and having children, if the Lord wills it for us; and then, to "retire from our arduous labors," so as to continue enjoying "the golden years of our lives!"

But understanding our mortality compels us and constrains us to "put things in perspective," with priorities "in the right order."

What really matters then? What really matters is: Our relationships with God and with each other! Such remembrances, experiences, and memories, a dying person will cherish in his or her heart, mind, soul, and spirit — we can't take any thing physical or material with us as we leave this world!

Thus, a life well-lived also includes caring for our fellow Human Beings in ways that demonstrate our love for God by the indwelling of His Holy Spirit. We continue to endure in this world, through the sealing of our heavenly inheritance from our redemptive salvation by Christ Jesus. (Romans 16:19–20; 1 Corinthians 10::13; Philippians 4:13).

"Truly, truly, I say to you, Before Abraham was, I am!" (John 8:58). This is an eternal Reality that we must take hold of in order to have the good courage to hang on to Life as prescribed and bolstered for us by God's loving kindness, grace, and Mercy. for Jesus was "in the flesh" when He uttered these prophetic words! So can we! For He said, "Greater things shall ye do because I go to the Father." (John 14:12–17).

God is with us always, through His Holy Spirit, in Christ Jesus who told us: "And lo, I am with you always, even unto the end of the world." (Matthew 28:18–20).

For example, will a dying man request to drive his Cadillac "one last time?" Rather, will he not pray and hope and desire that his wife, children, friends, neighbors, and/or family would come to be present by his side, visiting him for sincere well-wishing, for loving and uplifting encouragement, and for imparting to him a sense of having God's will and purpose to have had been fulfilled for the love of Christ in him, for his own benefit as well as for the well-being of his loved ones and for edifying the general welfare of his society during his earthly life time? Yes, for such blessings a dying man might desire, hope and pray!

Thinking through the problems we encounter and reconciling with obstacles we have to overcome while temporarily living on the Earth, are not an easy or comforting task. Our journey is fraught with ups-and-downs, uncertainties, unforeseen adversities, tempestuous storms, and moments of dashed hopes. (Matthew 6:24; 21:13; KJV).

Therefore, only our trust in God our heavenly Father through Christ's Holy Spirit can give us the strength to go on. (Philippians 4:13).

Only by our reliance on our faith in Christ can we overcome the stress of not knowing the future, even as we are, through love, enduring in all things, in the present, as "God's holy habitation," the Church, "the Israel of God," "the Body of Christ," even as each one of us, faithful believers in Christ Jesus, continues to live on the Earth as "the temple for God's Holy Spirit." (1 Corinthians Chapter 13; Ephesians 2:8–10; 13–22; Philippians 4:4–13; 19–23, KJV).

★★★

JESUS MAKES ALL THINGS RIGHT!

WITH THE NEW COVENANT, Jesus makes all things right! Every thing that "went wrong" under the Old Covenant as "a type and shadow of things to come," has been "made right," or has been "corrected" under the New Covenant, as Jesus Christ, the risen Lord and Savior, becomes the only foundation, the only substance for all the Scriptures. Jesus is the "climax of all Human History!" (Genesis 3:15; John 3:16; 10:7-18; 17:1-3; Romans 15:17-21; 1 Corinthians 3:9-17; Colossians 2:13-20; Hebrews 8:4-7; 10:1-10; Revelation 1:7-8; 17-18).

For "God is not a God of confusion but of peace as in all the churches of the saints." (Jeremiah 29:11; Matthew 5:9; 1 Corinthians 14:33).

"For I know the thoughts I think towards you, saith the Lord, THOUGHTS OF PEACE, and not of evil, to give you AN EXPECTED END." (Genesis 3:15; Deuteronomy 18:18-19; John 3:16; 8:31-36; 17:3; 16-26).

In the Garden of Eden, Adam and Eve disobeyed God's commandment, and Cain murders his own brother Abel after their parents were cast out of the Garden.

But in the Garden of Gethsemane, Jesus obeys God's Will by going to the Cross. And instead of Abel, it's the blood of Jesus that cleanses us from all sin. Abel's blood could not atone for us; nor could the blood of Isaac whom God saved from his father's knife. (Matthew 26:38-41; John 15:12-22; Hebrews 11:17-19; 12:22-29).

King Saul, the first King of "the children of Israel" (who are also, "the children of Jacob") was from the tribe of Benjamin; he was "chosen for his tall stature," but had lost God's blessing! SAUL is therefore "restored" through Saul of Tarsus, Hebrew of Hebrews, from the tribe of Benjamin, Roman Citizen, formerly "persecutor of Christians," and a Pharisee whose name Christ changes to Paul, Apostle of Christ Jesus who "confronted" him on the road to Damascus.

King Saul, "prefiguring" rebellion, usurpation, and disobedience, is "redeemed unto salvation" through forgiveness and redemption of the Apostle Paul, formerly "Saul of Tarsus." (Acts 9:1–18; 22:1–30; 26:12–18; Philippians 3:1–16).

Joseph, — "most favored" son of Jacob, the patriarch and father of the twelve tribes of "Israel," — sold into slavery by his own jealous and resentful brothers, but acquiring "a governing position" in Egypt, forgives his brothers, and welcomes the whole family of Jacob, whose name is also "Israel" his father, so that "the twelve tribes" could be "saved" for a Remnant through whom Jesus, from the Tribe of Judah, the root of Jesse, and the true heir of King David's throne for an everlasting reign, could be born of the Virgin Mary by the intervention of God's Holy Spirit; while Joseph, the Provider, — whose father is also named "Jacob," signifying that he is also "a son of Israel," —becomes the adoptive earthly father of baby Jesus, caring, along with Mary, for His upbringing, and needs for protection, safety, security, love, food, clothing, shelter, healthcare, and education.

This time, this Joseph, earthly adoptive father of our Lord Jesus, the "Emmanuel of God;" (Isaiah 9:6–7); yes, this same Joseph, the husband of the Virgin Marry; this very Joseph whose father's name was also "Jacob," (Matthew 1:16), was neither a slave, nor was he put in prison; nor is he put in a governing position "to lord it over" the Egyptians.

To the contrary, in the same manner that, for Jacob and the rest of the Tribes of Israel, Egypt was "a place of refuge" so that a Remnant could survive during the famine that stroke the whole land, Egypt, has also become a sanctuary for Joseph, the earthly father of Jesus, as provided by God for His Son Jesus, so as to be protected from the bloody swords of Herod who sent his soldiers into Ramah to kill all male children, two years old and under. (Hosea 11:1; Matthew 2:7–15).

Thus, God, the heavenly Provider for Christ our Savior, had "pre-positioned" His Son "between two Josephs," — between two Providers — Jesus' earthly father, Joseph, "the builder," the "carpenter," to provide for Him at His birth; and Joseph of Arimathea, a righteous rich man who was also waiting for God's kingdom, and thus, who also provided a freshly rock-hewn tomb for Jesus' burial: Thus, God made "provisions" through the two Josephs, "Providers for Jesus," so that Jesus would have all things He would need "in this world" as the "Son of Man," from His very conception

IT'S A CONTINUUM

and birth in the Holy Spirit, and also as "the Son of God! For, after His crucifixion and burial, Christ rose from the dead, as "the Son of God," to become "the God-sent Provider for all the living," as the God of eternal life, of liberty, of peace, of love, of grace and of Truth that sets us free; and thus, also as the God of "life more abundant." (Jeremiah 29:11; 31:31–34; John 3:16; 8:31–36; 10:7–11; John 17:3; Romans 8:1–17; 26–28; Galatians 5:1; 13; 1 Timothy 3:14–16; 2 Timothy 1:7; 2:8–9; 1 Peter 2:16; 1 John 3:8).

Mary, the Virgin mother of Christ, "restores" Eve, "mother of all the living;" Eve who was tempted and seduced by the Serpent's deceitful wiles. (Genesis 3:1–24). And, of course, Rebecca, Isaac's wife who persuaded Jacob, also "Israel," their younger son, in a scheme for him to "steal his older brother's birthright," Esau's birthright, so that Jacob, "the supplanter," could receive the blessing of Isaac, instead of Esau! Thus, Rebecca, is also "restored."

Hence, why "the Israel of God," the Church, "the Body of Christ," "the pillar and bulwark of the Truth," is called by God through Isaac, "the Seed of faith," and not through Jacob, "the schemer," "the supplanter."

But more than those, such women, the closest friends of Jesus, were the first to discover that Christ had risen from the dead, to then tell Peter and the other Disciples that the freshly rock-hewn grave was empty.

Thus, all women, from Eve to Mary Magdalene, were "restored by Christ" through the New Covenant of Love, forgiveness, and peace! (John 13:34–35; 20:11–18).

As Eve was "mother of all the living," so is, Mary is "mother of all the living," figuratively speaking, through Christ, her Son, who rose from the dead to give "spiritual rebirth" to newly born sons and daughters of God; but who, instead of being "cast out of Paradise," now, becomes "heirs with Christ" in the Kingdom of God, "according to the promise." (Genesis 3:1–24; Romans 8:12–17; Galatians 3:23–29).

For now, both men and women, young and old, could become "children of the Most High God," through their faith in Christ who "opened the Veil," as it was "rent in two" at His death on the Cross, so that "all the living" can have "bold access" to God's heavenly "holy of holies," to His "throne of grace." (2 Corinthians 3:7–18).

(Now, women no longer stood "disgraced" or "condemned" but were redeemed through love, friendship, and healing. Martha, Mary her sister, and Mary Magdalene became Jesus' "best friends," so much, that they are the first Humans who discovered that Jesus Christ had risen from the dead so as to inform the Disciples of that miraculous glorious event.)

Now, just as through Abraham, "father of faith," — by faith, through the Son of the living God, — every Human Being can receive God's blessing, without dissimulation, and without partiality, by simply accepting and believing on the name of Jesus Christ as Lord and Savior; thus, also by faith and for faith; from faith to faith, we all, in Christ Jesus, receive the Faith that "is the victory that overcomes the world," with liberty and freedom, for every one, for every Human Person who believes in Christ Jesus. (John 8:31-36; 14:6-27; 16:8-33; Romans 1:16-17; 1 John 4:13-19; 5:3-5).

"For God takes no bribes and shows no favoritism or partiality." (Deuteronomy 10:14-17; 2 Chronicles 19:7; Romans 2:6-11; 12:9; Galatians 2:3-7; Ephesians 6:9; Colossians 3:23-25; 1 Peter 1:14-17).

Because "Life is in the blood" (Leviticus 17:11), God had instituted "animal sacrifice," (Genesis 3:20-21), as a substitution for sin atonement, or for "prefiguring," what God would later accomplish through sending Christ Jesus to die in our place, shedding His holy precious blood to cleanse us of all sins, iniquities, transgressions and trespasses.(Genesis 3:15; Romans 10:8-13; Galatians 3:1-14; 2 Peter 1:1-11).

No one is good but God; our righteousness is "as filthy rags." No Human person, neither Abel nor Isaac, had qualified to become "the Savior of Humanity." God stopped Abraham from killing his own son, Isaac; and as Abraham looked around, he saw "a ram caught in the thicket" and it became the sacrifice, instead of Isaac. And there is something now that "speaks more graciously of better things than the blood of Abel:" The blood of the Son of the living God who had power to rise from the dead and to also raise the dead unto "new life," both "biologically and spiritually," to bring about "Zion," "the New Jerusalem from Heaven," "the New Heaven and the New Earth!" (Genesis: 22:9-14; Psalms 103:10-22: Isaiah 64:4-7; John 11:1-44; 12:1-2; Hebrews 8:10-13; 11:1-40; 12:22-24; 13:8; Revelation 21:1-27).

But Jesus Christ, perfect Son of Man from Adam and Eve to the Virgin Mary, and perfect Son of God through His Holy Spirit's "Immaculate Conception," as conceived by God's own Holy Spirit, lives forever.

Christ paid the price for our sins by giving up His own life as "a ransom for many," while, at the same time, — by His resurrection from the dead and ascension unto Heaven, — destroying the domain and rule of Satan,

IT'S A CONTINUUM

"the prince of this world," in heaven and on the Earth. (John12:31–36; 1 John 3:4–10).

"Where two of three are gathered in my name, so am I in the midst of you." (Matthew 18:18–20; 1 Corinthians 5:1–5).

God had worked through the Prophets upon whom He would interpose the Holy Spirit. Some people, like Enoch and Elijah entered Heaven directly to prove God's miraculous power and grace towards men accepted as "righteous" before the coming of Christ.

The last Prophet God had sent to announce and prepare the way for the appearing of Jesus, John the Baptist, was killed by Herod, then "the King of the children of Israel" during the times when the Roman Empire had conquered and occupied Palestine, and thus, Judea.

Physical-Geographical Jerusalem and the temple of stone were destroyed in 70 AD by the Roman General Titus, in fulfillment of Christ's prophecy, so that as prophesied in the Books of Isaiah and Hosea, God could "make a new thing." And in Jeremiah, God is doing "a new thing," so as to have "a Virgin in Israel," Mary, provide protection for the Son of Man, "God with us," Jesus, "Emmanuel of God."

But more, as prophesied, God would call out "His own children" to come from "a people who were not a people," and thus, to whom He would "give a new name:" The Apostles were first called "Christian" in Antioch, Syria. (Isaiah 43:18–19; Isaiah 62:2; Jeremiah 31:21–22; Hosea 2:21–23; Mark 13:1–2; Luke 21:1–9; Acts 11:19–30; Romans 9:19–29; 1 Peter 2:1–12).

And, during "Pentecost" that took place after the resurrection and ascension of Christ unto Heaven: The Apostles received "power from above" as prophesied by Christ. (Luke 24:45–49; Acts 2:1–11).

Jesus had sent "the Comforter," the Holy Spirit, as promised before His death, to now indwell and take residence within the spirit of all faithful believers who repent of their sins and confess Christ Jesus as Lord and Savior. Humans become "the temple" for God's Holy Spirit, to whom is given "a heart of flesh," rather let them wallow in harboring "a heart of stone." (Ezekiel 3:18–19; 36:26–27; 2 Corinthians 3:7–18).

Why is that significant? Because "The Law" was given on "tablets of stone," yielding a "temple of stone," as a place of worship, study, and prayer. But better yet, because no one could be justified by the Law while worshipping God in a temple of stone, then, "God's plan of Salvation" was that He would indwell Humans, and that Human Beings would become "a holy habitation" for His Holy Spirit through faith in Jesus Christ, the Savior, "Messiah," "the Chosen One," "The Anointed One."

As affirmed and testified by the Apostle Peter: "For we have not followed cunningly devised fables, when we made known unto you the power and coming of our Lord Jesus Christ, but were eyewitnesses of his majesty." (Matthew 3:13–17; 17:1–13; Mark 1:1–15; Luke 3:21–22; 2 Peter 1:16–21).

In spite of the fact that the "children of Israel" had been "a rebellious people," a "stiff-necked people," with "a heart of stone," now, God would send His own only begotten Son, through whom, the law would then be "written not with ink," but with God's Holy Spirit "on tablets of Human hearts." God has indeed "restored all power, authority, and dominion" unto Christ so that as His ambassadors and representatives on the Earth, we have no lack. For every thing that is God's also belongs to Christ and His heirs, which, we are through His shed blood that redeemed us from sin and hell, as confirmed by our faith in Jesus Christ. (Exodus 33:1–6; 34:8–9; Deuteronomy 9:6–29; Psalms 24:1; Isaiah 66:1–2; Jeremiah 31:21–37; Mark 13:1–2; John 16:8–15; 2 Corinthians 3:1–3).

God created the whole Universe, but only Humans, did he create "unto His own image and likeness." God did "something new" as prophesied by the Prophet Isaiah: We became "a holy habitation" for God's Holy Spirit, our very bodies taken from the dust of the ground of the Earth, rather than a "temple of stone" coming from "an accursed Earth" due to the sin of Adam and Eve. (Jeremiah 29:10–14; 1 Corinthians 3:16–23; Ephesians 2:11–22; 1 Peter 2:1–25).

Now with a "heart of flesh" and "the Law written on tablets of Human hearts" for the indwelling of God's Holy Spirit, we are no longer under the Law. We're now under Grace by the New Covenant of Love, so that our righteous works glorify God in Christ by our faith rather than by compulsory works as required by the Law of sin and death, which Jesus fulfilled by His death on the Cross. (Romans 2:12–29; 8:1–17; Hebrews 10:15–24).

The Priesthood, —Under the Old Covenant, begun with Aaron, from the tribe of Levi, "was stained" by his allowing "the children of Israel" to forge "a golden calf" to worship in the desert while Moses was obtaining the Ten Commandments on Mount Sinai, after which more than 23,000 perished in the desert in one day, — was now "restored," but "in the order of Melchizedek," priest and king of Salem, to whom Abram, later Abraham, "father of faith," had given "tithes of all things that he had," and with whom, he would also "break bread and drink wine," the very emblems of the Last

IT'S A CONTINUUM

Supper which Christ Jesus instituted as "communion" in remembrance of Him. (Genesis 14:18–20; Psalms 24:1; 127:1–2; Isaiah 66:1; Luke 22:14–23; 24:30–32; 1 Corinthians 10:1–13; 11:23–29).

What is physical is physical —- but "spiritual things are spiritually discerned." (1 Corinthians 2:6–16).

Jesus Christ, Son of Man, but Son of God, by the workings of God's Holy Spirit came out of the womb of the Virgin Mary; the "bag of waters" or "amniotic sac" was broken and water ran out during His birth. (1 John 5:6–12). God had destroyed the Earth through the great flood; but Noah and his family were "saved" through water. God will no longer destroy Humankind by water; now water is life; through baptism, we are saved through Jesus Christ, not for the removal of filth from the body, "but as the answer of a good conscience toward God," as a mark or seal for our faithful and obedient service to Christ our Lord. (1 Peter 3:8–22). Did not Pilate "wash his hands with water" in an attempt to exculpate himself of "guiltiness of blood," which he had acquired, by abdicating his judicial responsibilities, when saying, "I am innocent of the blood of this just man; see to it yourselves;" and by that, "allowing" the soldiers to crucify Christ on behalf of the Sanhedrin and the High Priest Caiaphas? (Matthew 27:24–26; John 18:12–14).

We had come from the dust of the ground of the Earth, now, with water present, Christ would use both to institute baptism by immersion. God would no longer use a great flood with water covering the whole Earth to destroy wicked Humans in order to restore faith and righteousness with the few people who had believed in Him. Water is Life! Full-immersion Baptism indicates "our seal for entrance" unto "life more abundant" and life Eternal: "Out of your hearts shall flow, rivers of living water." (Genesis 5:5–22; Proverbs 4:23; John 7:37–39; 1 Peter 3:8–22; 2 Peter 1:11; Revelation 22:14–21).

Humans, who were under a curse from the womb to the tomb since Adam and Eve, would now receive "God's indescribable gift:" Forgiveness of sins through salvation by Christ whose love "had bled at the Cross" for our sakes, but also for "life more abundant" and eternal life. (2 Corinthians 8:1–15; 9:11–15).

For Jesus was God, from the womb to the tomb: He was the only Son of God begotten of the Holy Spirit and He rose from the dead after His crucifixion and burial in the tomb bestowed by the rich man, Joseph of Arimathea.

JESUS MAKES ALL THINGS RIGHT!

God did "something new:" Given that Jesus was "the true Seed of Abraham," the "womb of Mary" would prefigure or foreshadow its "spiritual equivalence" with the "womb of the Earth," or the tomb within which Jesus was placed after His death on the Cross. Jesus, the Seed of Abraham, Seed of promise, Seed of faith, "the True Vine," was thus, so to speak, "planted," in order to rise from the ground and "bear fruit" in its due season, unto Eternal Life, with the "glorious liberty of the children of God." As Christ had exited the Virgin Mary's womb as the Son of Man and the Son of God to then be "the light of the world" who brings life with Him as "the bread of life," so too, by His resurrection from the grave, Jesus signifies "the Seed of Abraham" that was "planted" coming out of the earth as "the true Vine" from which we, Christians, "as the branches," would obtain "life more abundant" and eternal life, as well as power from the Holy Spirit for enlightening the world that is "in darkness of sin" due to Satan being "the prince of this world." (John 15:1–11; Romans 8:18–25).

Now, the resurrection of Christ gives "spiritual rebirth" through the indwelling of His Holy Spirit in us, as "the law" is now "written on tablets of Human hearts." The Law, "as a custodian," or "as task-master," no longer has "power over us:" For we are now under Grace! We do what is right in the sight of God, not out of compulsion or fear of deadly punishment, but because we are "the righteousness of God," loved for an everlasting inheritance," through Christ Jesus our risen Lord and Savior. (Jeremiah 31:33; Ezekiel 34:15–16; 36:26–28; 2 Corinthians 3:1–3).

We now "have the Mind of Christ" with which "to reason spiritually" as inspired by Godly wisdom and the Holy Spirit as a "discerner of the thoughts of the heart" to not only guide us unto understanding and knowledge of God's Word in Christ Jesus but to also "re-discover" the eternal truths that Christ told us the Holy Spirit would reveal to us, because Jesus is "the way, the truth and the life." (Isaiah 1:11–18; John 14:6–7; 1 Corinthians 2:6–16; Hebrews 4:11–13).

Through Adam we all died biologically with no hope for eternal life! (Genesis 3:17–24). But through Jesus Christ we live forever, even as we are only "passing through" in this biological body on the Earth whose mortality is only a miraculous opportunity to enter into "eternal life" through Christ Jesus, King of kings and Lord of lords, who rose from the dead, ascended unto Heaven and is returning for us to reign with Him at the right hand of power of God in Heaven and on Earth — in a new Heaven and a new Earth, as promised by God through His Prophets whose prophesies are fulfilled

IT'S A CONTINUUM

in Christ Jesus, the living Son of the living God! (Romans 2:6-11; 27-29; 3:21-26; 1 Corinthians 14:33; 2 Corinthians 3:1-6; 10:3-6).

Through our "priest" in "the order of Melchizedek," Jesus Christ who had offered Himself as a propitiation for our sins, we are now "a royal priesthood of believers," who are also "kings, priests, and prophets," all in one, as we have been "born again," from "babes in Christ" unto "a chosen generation," now as mature adults made-ready for "the bread of eternal life," as faithful representatives and "ambassadors of Christ," the Son of God, on the Earth. (2 Corinthians 5:9-21; Hebrews 5:7-14; 7:11-12; 1 Peter 2:1-10, KJV).

We have bold entrance through Christ before God's Holy Throne of Grace; His flesh had died as the veil in "the temple of stone" was "rent in two" to open the entrance to "the holy of holies" where the "arc of the Covenant" was to be kept, but which is now in Heaven. Thus, through the blood of Jesus and His resurrection power, we have direct access to our heavenly Father who planted "the tree of life" for us, seal of which, only Christ could open. (Mark 15:37-39; 2 Corinthians 3:7-18; Ephesians 3:7-12; Hebrews 12:1-2; Revelation 6:1-17).

SEED becomes fruit tree — Abraham's Seed, Christ Jesus, and now also us, as heirs with Christ in God's kingdom — Christ, buried, now risen as "the first fruit of the dead," who, as "the Seed of faith," was planted into "the accursed ground," now "washed in His blood," pure Holy righteous blood, as a redemption from the curse of Adam; yes, Jesus, "the last Adam" has arisen from the dead, to bear the first fruits of the Spirit, and then spread "its branches" as the Vine, from whom all faithful believers gain "life more abundant," and eternal life. (Genesis 3: 17-24; John 6:35-40; Romans 8:18-25; 1 Corinthians 15:42-50).

How does that apply to our world of which "Satan is the prince?" Satan is a defeated foe whose head has been "bruised" as prophesied in Genesis 3:15; for, as "priests, kings, and prophets," we become the "elect" in both Heaven and on the Earth, the true real heirs of God's kingdom in Christ Jesus — For example, America is hence "a miracle," where we, "the electors," "We the voters," choose our Representatives and Senators, and President of the United States, as "public servants" into the halls of government office. Our government was established, not before, but after we received our true freedoms from our God-endowed lives and Liberty for the "pursuit of Happiness." Our inalienable Rights from our Creator came, first, before government was "created" by America's Founding Fathers. (Declaration of

JESUS MAKES ALL THINGS RIGHT!

Independence, 1776; Constitution of the United States of America, 1787; First Elected President of the United States, 1789: George Washington, the former General who, at the close of the Revolutionary War against the British Empire in 1783, returned to his farm to plant and harvest his crops; First Ten Amendments of our Constitutional Bill of Rights, 1791).

Still, we are "citizens of Heaven" awaiting the "Jerusalem from Heaven" which Christ will bring into being when He returns. "The earth is the Lord's and the fullness thereof," what does it profit a man "to gain the whole world but lose his soul?" We die; we pass away; we can't own God's property, except, "some of it," by His beloved design through laws and regulations He allows us to institute. (Ephesians 2:11–22; Hebrews 11:1–2; 10–13; 16).

"Heaven is my throne and the earth is my footstool" (Psalms 24:1; 127:1–2; Isaiah 66:1) — Hence, why Jesus appealed to ALL Humanity, "sheep that were not yet of his flock" when He was on the Earth! (Mark 15:37–39; John 3:1–16; 4:7–28; 10:14–18; Acts 10:1–43; 44–48).

We, its inhabitants, belong to God, and thus, that the whole Planet be filled with His children, indwelled by His Holy Spirit as we wait for "the heavenly Jerusalem," a "better country," where the arc of the Covenant is already and of which geographical Jerusalem, whose name has never changed, was "the symbol" foreshadowing "the city on a hill," "the city of the Great King" that God through Christ King of kings and Lord of lords will then establish for us as a "New heaven and a New earth." (Psalms 24:1–2; 48:1–2; Isaiah 66:1; Matthew 5:33–37; 1 Timothy 6:14–16; Hebrews 11:16; Revelation 11–19; 19:11–16; 20:21).

Thus, as we are "children of the promise" from the Seed of Abraham's faith whom God made "father of many nations," we have the whole Earth, "not for a possession," —because "the fullness thereof" belongs to God, (Psalms 24), and thus, because "we leave every thing behind" when we die, — but as "the fields" that are "made ready for harvest" in order that all people-groups, "tongues, tribes and nations," might receive the opportunity to know Jesus as Lord and Savior, for a miraculous rejoicing in heaven and on Earth, even "for one sinner who repents!" (Matthew 9:35–38; Luke 15:3–7; John 4:34–38; Acts 2:1–21; Revelation 1:4–8; 7:9–10; 11:1–11).

We were created unto the image and likeness of God, "a little lower than God Himself," "a little lower than the angels," so that, through the coming of Christ, we might learn how to live in Christ-likeness, as God Himself would live, were He to take the form of a Human Being again!

Jesus is "the prince of peace" and where He reigns, there is love, there is peace, and there is justice where "all the good that is ours in Christ Jesus" takes form, is molded unto creation, fashioned unto a divine congregation, whose all members now belong to the same Body, the Church, "the Body of Christ," "the pillar and bulwark of the Truth," the Truth of God in Christ Jesus that has already "set us free." (John 8:31–36; 1 Timothy 3:14–16).

Many people, children, young and old, are waiting to become "adopted sons and daughters of God," to be "grafted unto the Vine" who is Jesus Christ, through God's Holy Spirit; Christ, "the first fruit risen from the dead," so as to also be transformed in spirit, heart, mind and soul, unto "ambassadors of Christ" doing God's righteous "works of faith" on the Earth, for the benefit of all Humankind! (Mark 10:13–16; Luke 18:15–17; 2 Corinthians 5:12–21).

But more, from the Samaritan woman at Jacob's well to "the good Samaritan," from Saul of Tarsus, now, the Apostle Paul, to you and me, forgiveness for "newness of life" awaits all Humanity from whom the "predestined elect of God" shall issue! (Matthew 10:26–28; Luke 10:25–37; 17:11–19; John 4:7–26; 10:7–18; Romans 8:28–30; Philippians 4:19–23).

"One flock!" "One Shepherd!" For Jesus Christ is Lord! Let His name and Spirit reverberate throughout the whole world as Savior and God of all Humankind! Come again soon, Lord Jesus, King of kings and Lord of lords! Glory to God in Jesus' Name! Hallelujah! Amen! (John 10:7–18; 1 Corinthians 14:33, KJV; 2 Corinthians 5:14–21; Revelation 21:1–4; 22–27; 22:1–7; 12–21).

***

www.ingramcontent.com/pod-product-compliance
Lightning Source LLC
Chambersburg PA
CBHW070920160426
43193CB00011B/1535